BRITISH AND IRISH AUTHORS

Introductory Critical Studies

OSCAR WILDE

Oscar Wilde's personality, and the tragedy of his trials and imprisonment, can stand in the way of an appreciation of his literary achievement.
He was always a fashionable and controversial writer. Dismissed at first
as a populariser of other men's ideas, and later as essentially light-weight,
even trivial, Wilde has increased in reputation during recent years.
Some features of his writing – for instance, his exploration of unusual
forms like the prose-poem and the dance-drama, or his experiments with
traditional vehicles such as melodrama or fairy-tales – now seem
characteristically modern. Wilde's versatility, the lightness of his touch,
and the brilliance of his style, are facets of an originality and commitment
to art which was wholly serious but rarely solemn.

This new introductory study argues that Wilde's output should be
judged as a developing and unified whole, and that the element which
contributes most to this sense of unity is the inherently dramatic nature
of much of his work. Such a perspective places a high value on Wilde's
plays, and sees them as important within the development of modern
drama as well as for their intrinsic qualities.

BRITISH AND IRISH AUTHORS
Introductory critical studies

In the same series:

OSCAR WILDE

PETER RABY

Principal Lecturer and Head of English and Drama
Homerton College, Cambridge

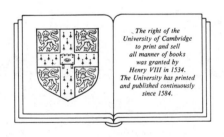

The right of the
University of Cambridge
to print and sell
all manner of books
was granted by
Henry VIII in 1534.
The University has printed
and published continuously
since 1584.

CAMBRIDGE UNIVERSITY PRESS

CAMBRIDGE

NEW YORK NEW ROCHELLE

MELBOURNE SYDNEY

Published by the Press Syndicate of the University of Cambridge
The Pitt Building, Trumpington Street, Cambridge CB2 1RP
32 East 57th Street, New York, NY 10022, USA
10 Stamford Road, Oakleigh, Melbourne 3166, Australia

British Library cataloguing in publication data
Raby, Peter, *1939–*
Oscar Wilde. – (British and Irish authors).
1. English literature. Wilde, Oscar – Critical
studies
I. Title   II. Series
828'809

Library of Congress cataloguing in publication data
Raby, Peter.
Oscar Wilde / Peter Raby.
p.   cm. – (British and Irish authors : introductory critical
studies)
Bibliography: p.
ISBN 0–521–26078–7. ISBN 0–521–27826–0 (pbk.)
1. Wilde, Oscar, 1854–1900 – Criticism and interpretation.
I. Title.   II. Series: British and Irish authors.
PR5824.R3 1988
828'.809–dc 19   88–2610

ISBN 0 521 26078 7 hard covers
ISBN 0 521 27826 0 paperback

GG

Contents

Preface

This introduction to Wilde's writing is based on a conviction that dramatic form, and the dramatic mode, are the unifying factors in his work. This is not to undervalue his earlier work, although such a perspective may not fully recognise his originality as a critic; rather, I argue that Wilde was in the process of discovering the artistic context which best matched his genius and temperament when society effectively silenced him. Deprived of the public arena and barred access to the stage, he was forced towards the intensely subjective but still inherently dramatic form of *De Profundis* and *The Ballad of Reading Gaol*. Qualities which make Wilde enjoyable for me include his accessibility, his command of narrative and his versatile use of popular forms, as well as the elegance of his style. I hope that I have reflected that sense of pleasure.

My general debts to previous critics are reflected in the notes and bibliography. I have been helped immeasurably by the two volumes of letters edited by Rupert Hart-Davis. Two books which have given me particular insights are *Oscar Wilde, Art and Egotism* by Rodney Shewan, and Katharine Worth's study of Wilde's plays. I regret that I have not had a chance to read Richard Ellmann's long-awaited biography, though I suspect that it may cause a severe attack of writer's block. In a study of this length it has not been possible to do more than indicate the outlines of Wilde's extraordinary life. The more I learn, the more I respect Wilde's achievement.

Chronology

1854, 16 October	Born in Dublin
1864–71	Portora Royal School, Enniskillen
1871–74	Trinity College, Dublin
1874, October	Magdalen College, Oxford
1875, June	Travel in Italy
1877, March–April	Travel in Greece and Italy
1878	Wins Newdigate Prize with poem 'Ravenna', completes degree with First in Greats
1881	*Poems* published
1882	Lecture tour of U.S.A. and Canada
1883, January–May	In Paris
August–September	In New York for production of *Vera*
September	Lectures in U.K.
26 November	Engaged to Constance Lloyd
1884, 29 May	Married in London
1885, 1 January	Moves into 16, Tite Street, Chelsea
5 June	Elder son Cyril born
1886, 3 November	Younger son Vyvyan born
1887–9	Editor, *Woman's World*
1888, May	*The Happy Prince and other Tales* published
1889, July	*The Portrait of Mr W. H.* (Blackwood's)
1890, June	*The Picture of Dorian Gray* (Lippincott's)
1891	Meets Lord Alfred Douglas
January	*The Duchess of Padua – 'Guido Ferranti' –* produced in New York
February	*The Soul of Man under Socialism* (fortnightly)
April	Extended version of *The Picture of Dorian Gray* published
May	*Intentions* published
July	*Lord Arthur Savile's Crime and Other Stories* published
November	*A House of Pomegranates* published
November–Dec.	Writes *Salomé* in Paris
1892, February	*Lady Windermere's Fan* produced
June	*Salomé* banned by Lord Chamberlain
1893, February	*Salomé* published in French
April	*A Woman of No Importance* produced

viii

November	*Lady Windermere's Fan* published
1894, February	*Salomé* published in English
June	*The Sphinx* published
October	*A Woman of No Importance* published
1895, January	*An Ideal Husband* produced
14 February	*The Importance of Being Earnest* produced
28 February	Finds Queensberry's card at Albemarle Club
5 April	Acquittal of Queensberry, arrest of Wilde
25 May	Sentenced after his second trial to two years' hard labour, imprisoned at Pentonville
4 July	Transferred to Wandsworth
20 November	Transferred to Reading
1896, February	Death of his mother, Lady Wilde; *Salomé* produced in Paris
1897, January–March	Writes *De Profundis*
19 May	Released from prison; crosses to Dieppe. Lives in France, Italy, Sicily and Switzerland until his death
1898, February	*The Ballad of Reading Gaol* published
7 April	Death of Constance Wilde
1899, February	*The Importance of Being Earnest* published
July	*An Ideal Husband* published
1900, 30 November	Dies in Hôtel d'Alsace, Paris

1

Introduction

The relationship between Oscar Wilde's life and his art, as represented by his literary work, makes complex and insistent demands on our attention. Wilde's life was, ostensibly at least, a highly public and publicised affair. Indeed, for five years or so between leaving Oxford in 1879 and marrying Constance Lloyd in 1884, Wilde's public image formed his principal claim to interest: these were the years of his North American and British lecture tours, the years when he frequented the *salons* of London and Paris, years when he channelled his energies into a seemingly relentless campaign of self-promotion. Apart from the lectures, Wilde wrote little at this time for publication except poetry. The following decade, by contrast, was a period of intense literary activity. Spurred on by the need to provide for his wife and two sons, Wilde accomplished the bulk of an amazingly varied and distinctive *oeuvre*: the short stories and tales, the critical essays, *The Picture of Dorian Gray, Salomé*, the three society comedies and *The Importance of Being Earnest*, besides undertaking the editorship of *Woman's World* and writing a substantial number of reviews, and occasional journalism. In addition to and parallel to this public career, he met first Robert Ross and, five years later, Lord Alfred Douglas, so initiating a phase of 'private' homosexual relationships, private in so far as they could not be openly acknowledged. Some of what Wilde wrote at the time seems to comment on this secretive, forbidden world, especially *The Portrait of Mr W. H.* and *The Picture of Dorian Gray*; other work, such as *The Importance of Being Earnest*, is susceptible to interpretation in this light; while certain pervasive motifs and preoccupations of Wilde, notably the idea of the artist–criminal, prepare the way for the later revelations.

In 1895, there erupted the scandalous sequence which is inclined to dominate our received concept of Wilde: the three trials, the bankruptcy, the vindictive prison sentence. Out of these terrible episodes, which were humiliating to Wilde, destructive to his wife and children, and incidentally a bleak indictment of English society, issued *De Profundis* and *The Ballad of Reading Gaol*, which, with some caveats (for nothing with Wilde is absolutely straightforward), represent direct reactions to Wilde's personal experience. There followed the three and a half years of exile, passed restlessly, and in increasing ill-health and anxiety about money, between France, Switzerland and Italy.

Wilde consistently viewed his own life in terms of art, though the definition of those terms passed through two major phases. In the period of his youth and success, he strove to live artistically and beautifully. The text he learned from Pater, 'To burn always with this hard, gemlike flame, to maintain this ecstasy, is success in life',[1] was applied to the mundane actions of daily life, and particularly to his physical surroundings, since these were more easily controllable. His desire was that everything should make a beautiful statement. From this impulse stemmed Wilde's perfecting of the most ephemeral of arts, that of conversation, as did his persistent obsession with dress and decoration. His description of the dandy, Lord Goring, in *An Ideal Husband*, provides a context where the aesthetic cult is perceived as a governing principle: 'One sees that he stands in immediate relation to modern life, makes it indeed, and so masters it. He is the first well-dressed philosopher in the history of thought.'[2] Lord Goring masters not only his own life but those of the other characters in the play, and by extension the composition of the British Cabinet; with an entirely new buttonhole, he leaves the stage for a private and domestic career. That image, the image of the idealised dandy, projected from the stage of the Theatre Royal, Haymarket in January 1895, heralds the close of Wilde's conspicuous attempts to express inner wisdom and beauty by means of the external. The triumph of the first night of *The Importance of Being Earnest*, the trivial play 'written by a butterfly for butterflies',[3] was marred by Lord Queensberry's ominous proximity, prowling round the St James's Theatre with his grotesque tribute of a bouquet of vegetables. Nothing that came after in Wilde's life could be described as aesthetic.

In the two years of imprisonment which followed the public humiliation of the trials, all the things which Wilde had chosen to surround himself with – clothes, pictures, wine, buttonholes – were removed from him. Deprived of the decorative, he chose now to reflect on his life in terms of drama, an appropriate metaphor for him to adopt since he had achieved his greatest public recognition as a dramatist, and since it was arguably the form which he understood most instinctively and acutely. There are two passages in *De Profundis*, itself a kind of dramatic monologue, where Wilde explores this decision to perceive his own life as drama. The first is his recollection of the occasion, during the bankruptcy proceedings, when a solictor's clerk leaned across the table and said in a low voice, 'Prince Fleur-de-Lys wishes to be remembered to you.' (Such a scene, and line, in a Wilde play might send a commentator to the well-made *boulevard* plays of Sardou or Dumas *fils* in search of a precedent.) Wilde comments to Douglas: 'I saw – and subsequent events showed me that I rightly saw – that nothing that had happened had made you realise a single thing. You were in your own eyes still the graceful prince of a trivial comedy, not the sombre figure of a tragic show.'[4]

The emergence of Wilde as a tragic figure, and his awareness of his tragic dimension, with all the implications of that claim, reveal a clear structure within both his life and his work. As he wrote in a second and later passage in *De Profundis*: 'I remember I used to say [in 'The Critic As Artist'] that I thought I could bear a real tragedy if it came to me with purple pall and a mask of noble sorrow, but that the dreadful thing about modernity was that it put Tragedy into the raiment of Comedy, so that the great realities seemed commonplace or grotesque or lacking in style.'[5] To illustrate the grotesque tragi-comic mode, Wilde describes his appearance in transit from Wandsworth to Reading Gaol:

Everything about my tragedy has been hideous, mean, repellent, lacking in style. Our very dress makes us grotesques. We are the zanies of sorrow. We are clowns whose hearts are broken. We are specially designed to appeal to the sense of humour. On November 13th 1895 I was brought down here from London. From two o'clock till half-past two on that day I had to stand on the centre platform of Clapham Junction in convict dress and handcuffed, for the world to look at. I had been taken out of the Hospital Ward without a moment's notice being given to me. Of all possible objects I was the most grotesque. When people saw me they laughed. Each train as it came up swelled the audience. Nothing could exceed their amusement. That was of course before they knew who I was. As soon as they had been informed, they laughed still more. For half an hour I stood there in the grey November rain surrounded by a jeering mob.[6]

In *De Profundis*, the archetype of Christ is never far from Wilde's consciousness; but in passages such as the above he seems simultaneously to be reshaping his experiences in the form of a modern tragic drama such as Ibsen's. Wilde in his life, or in his account of his life, was reflecting his own principle: 'A Truth in

art is that whose contradictory is also true';[7] the period of
graceful, artificial comedy is fulfilled by the grotesque bitterness of
modern tragedy. In 'The Decay of Lying' Wilde had argued that
Life imitated Art far more than Art imitated Life. In *De Profundis*,
Wilde looked back over his life and art and concluded that the
tragic mask was necessary for him. He recalled a June morning
in Oxford, his pre-lapsarian paradise, when he told a friend that
he wanted 'to eat of the fruit of all the trees in the garden of the
world', and that he was going out into the world with that passion
in his soul:

My only mistake was that I confined myself so exclusively to the trees of
what seemed to me the sun-gilt side of the garden, and shunned the other
side for its shadow and its gloom. Failure, disgrace, poverty, sorrow,
despair, suffering, tears even, the broken words that come from the lips
of pain, remorse that makes one walk in thorns, conscience that condemns, self-abasement that punishes, the misery that puts ashes on its
head, the anguish that chooses sackcloth for its raiment and into its own
drink puts gall – all these were things of which I was afraid. And as I
had determined to know nothing of them, I was forced to taste each one
of them in turn, to feed on them, to have for a season, indeed, no other
food at all. I don't regret for a single moment having lived for pleasure.
I did it to the full, as one should do everything that one does to the full.
There was no pleasure that I did not experience. I threw the pearl of my
soul into a cup of wine. I went down the primrose path to the sound of
flutes. I lived on honeycomb. But to have continued the same life would
have been wrong because it would have been limiting. I had to pass on.
The other half of the garden had its secrets for me also.
Of course all this is foreshadowed and prefigured in my art.[8]

Wilde proceeds to cite instances of the motif of suffering, the note
of doom, which may be discerned in 'The Happy Prince', 'The
Young King', 'The Picture of Dorian Gray', 'The Critic as
Artist', 'The Soul of Man under Socialism', *Salomé*. Artistically,
Wilde recognised the necessity of entering the spiritual crucible of
Brand after the explorations of *Peer Gynt*.

In Rodney Shewan's definition, 'Wilde devoted his career to in-
vestigating that most elusive of subject matter, the self, and
creating an expressive medium for his findings.'[9] Wilde used
Life, his own life and experience, as material for his Art: the
characteristic capital letters, arresting in their pretension, give
ample notice of his formal intention. Wilde's attitude to art is a
comparatively rare phenomenon within English culture, confined
principally to the first flush of Romanticism (aside from its late,
decadent flowering). In its manifestations through Keats, Shelley

and, in a different way, Byron, it is somehow made more acceptable by the accompaniment of scandal, exile and early death, all
to be part of Wilde's lot. The English do not like to be seen to take
art seriously; they like even less an artist who appears to take
himself seriously, though, perhaps understandably, they failed to
see that it was his art first, and his self secondly and effectively as
a constituent of that art, which Wilde sought to promote.

If Wilde formulated any one model of the Artist, it was based
on Keats, who embodied most of the necessary qualifications:
poetic genius, physical beauty, public persecution, an early death.
Diverted from Rome by his Dublin tutor Mahaffy, Wilde's receptive powers had been heightened by all the associations, the
'idyllic loveliness',[10] of Greece; he returned to England via Rome
in the spring of 1877. The imaginative and emotional pressure was
intense: in rapid succession he found himself kneeling before
Pope Pius IX at the instigation of his friend Hunter-Blair, and
then paying homage, a mourner obedient to Shelley's invocation
in *Adonais*, at Keats's grave. The experience was reflected in a
sonnet which he despatched to Lord Houghton, Keats's bio-
grapher and editor, urging him to mount a campaign for a
suitable memorial. Wilde also wrote a monograph, *The Tomb of
Keats*, which appeared first in the *Irish Monthly* for July 1877. As
he wrote to Lord Houghton, in a letter whose phrasing echoes that
of the article, 'Someway standing by his grave I felt that he too
was a Martyr, and worthy to lie in the city of Martyrs. I thought
of him as a Priest of Beauty slain before his time, a lovely Sebastian killed by the arrows of a lying and unjust tongue.'[11] Wilde's
self-consciously deprecatory descriptions – a 'boyish poem' (of
the sonnet), and 'little more than a stray sheet from a boy's diary'
(of the monograph) – suggest that he identified strongly with
Keats's poetic vocation: 'a Priest of Beauty slain before his time'.
It is also clear that Wilde was, even at this early stage of his life
(though not early by comparison with Keats's example), an
acolyte to the Priesthood of Beauty.

Wilde's whole life, in fact, evolved as a conscious process of self-
expression, and particularly of self-dramatisation. He saw his role
as an artist in terms of a vocation, one which became, for him, impossible to reconcile with social convention. His comment on
Tennyson defines the distance between the sacred calling of the
artist and the occupation of the Victorian family man: 'How can
a man be a great poet and lead the life of an English country-
gentleman? Think of a man going down to breakfast at eight

o'clock with the family, and writing *Idylls of the King* until lunch-time.'[12] Wilde's concept of the artist envisaged a much more public and active role, in which his own voice and physical presence were essential components of his art. Wilde, of course, acquired many 'voices', personae and masks, which enabled him to operate across a wide range of tones. Some of the more notable were the *salon* conversationalist, the connoisseur and the public lecturer. Like a good actor, he habitually demonstrated an instinctive awareness of his audience, whether in a private or public context. In much of his writing, too, the notion of the speaking voice is prominent: behind the tales one is conscious of the voice of the story-teller; in the critical dialogues and the drama the form itself acknowledges and exploits the oral medium; and the same acknowledgement is present, in a different way, in the examples of the confessional letter *De Profundis* and *The Ballad of Reading Gaol*.

The relationship between Wilde's life, his self and his work is one that occupied and perplexed many of his friends. One interesting testimony to this comes from the journals of Charles Ricketts, an artist and critic whose belief in beauty was 'held as seriously as any moral convictions of the mid-Victorians'.[13] Ricketts's comments were prompted by his going to see a revival of *An Ideal Husband* (they also incidentally introduce another critical minefield, Wilde's attitude towards his own work):

I was surprised to find it much better than I had thought. I remember Oscar saying of it, when he insisted on our being present at the first night: 'It was written for ridiculous puppets to play, and the critics will say, "Ah, here is Oscar unlike himself!" – though in reality I became engrossed in writing it, and it contains a great deal of the real Oscar.' This is a final and a severe estimate of it. Oscar was always better than he thought he was, and no one in his lifetime was able to see it, including my clairvoyant self. It is astonishing that I viewed him as the most genial, kindly, and civilized of men, but it never entered my head that his personality was the most remarkable one that I should ever meet, that in intellect and humanity he is the largest type I have come across. Other greater men of my time were great in some one thing, not large in their very texture.[14]

Ricketts was a friend whom Wilde admired and supported; his, remarked Wilde, was 'the one house in London where you will never be bored'. His brilliant work as designer or illustrator for *The Picture of Dorian Gray*, *A House of Pomegranates*, *Poems*, *The Sphinx* and *The Ballad of Reading Gaol* reveals deep understanding and

6

sympathy for Wilde's work. It is more significant, however, to note how Ricketts's estimate of Wilde is not only maintained but increased in the light of the art and literature of the early twentieth century. In 1919 Ricketts was still responding to *Salomé*, working on a proposed production for Tokyo. The 'large' texture of Wilde and his work seems to demand continual re-appraisal.

A comparable re-appraisal, or re-adjustment, to Wilde's work is that of André Gide, whose French perspective has particular illumination for a writer so attuned himself to French literature and art. In the foreword to the 1951 edition of his *Oscar Wilde*, Gide wrote:

> It seems to me today that in my first essay I spoke of Oscar Wilde's work, and in particular of his plays, with unjust severity. The English as well as the French led me to do this, and Wilde himself at times showed an amusing disdain for his comedies by which I allowed myself to be taken in. I admit that for a long time I therefore believed that *An Ideal Husband* and *A Woman of No Importance* were not to be regarded as anything but dramatic entertainment which was itself 'of no importance'. To be sure I have not come to consider these plays as perfect works; but they appear to me, today when I have learned to know them better, as among the most curious, the most significant and, whatever may have been said about them, the newest things in the contemporary theatre.[15]

Gide knew Wilde at three periods of his life. He met him for the first time in 1891 in Paris, when Wilde was enjoying the height of his success; he came across him again in Algeria in January 1895, together with Lord Alfred Douglas, as he records in *If It Die*; finally, he saw Wilde in the guise of Sebastian Melmoth when he went back to France on his release from prison. Gide's first judgment was that Wilde was not a great writer. Building on Wilde's much-quoted analysis, made to him in Algeria in January 1895, 'I have put all my genius into my life; I have put only my talent into my works',[16] Gide proposed for Wilde a different claim: 'A great writer, no, but a great *viveur*, if the word may be permitted to take on its full meaning. Like the philosophers of Greece, Wilde did not write but talked and lived his wisdom, imprudently entrusting it to the fluid memory of men, as if inscribing it on water.'[17] It is appropriate for the romantically inclined and classically educated Wilde both to emphasise the separation of art from life, and, paradoxically, to reverse the anticipated hierarchy. Gide appears to endorse Wilde's judgment, first by a comment, echoed by many contemporaries, that the best of Wilde's writing was 'only a pale reflection of his brilliant conversation'.[18] This comment may be true, though it is difficult to assess, since neither Gide's nor others' recollections of Wilde's conversation have consistently distinctive qualities which mark them as superior to Wilde's own writing. Gide's endorsement seems even less convincing when placed beside the passages about Wilde in *If It Die*, which describe Wilde's relationship with Douglas and the 'debauching' of Gide himself. Gide asserts that, with him, 'Wilde had now thrown aside his mask. It was the man himself I saw at last.'[19] There is a temptation, with a subject who consciously adopts so many poses and masks, for an individual to assume that he is privileged to reveal 'the man himself'. An alternative response is to refuse to resolve the tension between art and life, literature and conversation, or, at the personal level, a London drawing-room and an Arab café.

Gide's reference to the philosophers of Greece indicates an approach to the tension expressed by Wilde's characteristically balanced disclaimer. The role of the philosopher, especially the philosopher as teacher, was highly suited to Wilde's temperament and linguistic genius. His vocation as an artist demanded that the process of self-expression and self-dramatisation should be public and active, and his physical appearance and voice, or voices, were important elements of his art. He was a remarkable and early exponent of performance art. There are many isolated instances of Wildean acts and attitudes, notably among the Romantics; the idea of the dandy expresses intensely, in a restricted sphere, the Wildean perspective. But no one else in the nineteenth century devoted himself so openly and relentlessly to living his art. If friends found it confusing to reconcile the man and his work, it was because he used himself both so pervasively and yet so subtly to project it. A further quotation from Gide throws light on one of Wilde's artistic methods:

One morning Wilde handed me an article to read in which a rather dull-witted critic congratulated him for 'knowing how to invent pleasant tales the better to clothe his thought.' They believe, Wilde began, that all thoughts are born naked . . . They don't understand that I *cannot* think otherwise than in stories. The sculptor doesn't try to translate his thoughts into marble; *he thinks in marble*, directly.[20]

The story-teller is a crucial mode for Wilde as philosopher/artist/ poet. Many of his published tales began as less formal entertainments; in the final phase of his career, he was re-working the events of his own life into narrative, in *De Profundis* and *The Ballad of Reading Gaol*. The moral implications, or at the least bearing, of

INTRODUCTION

the stories form part of a tradition which is oral in origin. Wilde, acutely aware of his 'live' audience, individual or collective, transferred his instinct to control an audience's response into the sphere of his published work. It is this impulse, as much as his aesthetic sensibility, which shows itself in the minute attention to detail in Wilde's suggestions for type-face, paper and decoration in the editions of his books, and in the lengthy, almost obsessive letter campaigns that he conducted in the public press against his critics. At his three trials, by taking his place in the witness box, Wilde attempted to defend not only the conduct of his life but his concept of art. One among many perspectives from which *De Profundis* may be viewed is as the speech Wilde was refused permission to deliver when he received his sentence. By then, there was no place for any other story than his own.

A different kind of difficulty in confronting Wilde's range of masks and tones is that of recognising, or isolating, his individual voice. The extent to which Wilde reflected, echoed, indeed blatantly imitated, the ideas, forms and language of others has been variously described. An early instance was Oliver Elton's proposal that the Oxford Union should reject Wilde's presentation copy of his poems:

It is not that these poems are thin – and they are thin. It is not that they are immoral – and they are immoral: it is not that they are this or that – and they are all this and all that: it is that they are for the most part not by their putative father at all, but by a number of better-known and more deservedly reputed authors. They are, in fact, by Philip Sidney, by John Donne, by Lord Byron, by William Morris, by Algernon Swinburne and by sixty more whose works have furnished the list of passages which I hold at this moment . . .[21]

Certainly Wilde's early poems display a pervasive dependence upon a wide range of writers. The charge, in Elton's terms amounting to plagiarism, surfaces throughout Wilde's career. Wilde's often quoted and uncharacteristically unguarded remark to Whistler, 'I wish I had said that, Jimmy', and Whistler's reply 'You will, Oscar, you will', became a standard critique of Wilde for both contemporary and later commentators. Wilde's ideas on art are judged to be an undigested amalgam of, from the English tradition, Ruskin, Whistler, Morris and Pater; and, from the French, of Gautier, Baudelaire and Flaubert; *The Picture of Dorian Gray* is seen to derive from Huysmans and Pater; *Salomé* is dismissed as a pallid imitation of Flaubert and Maeterlinck; the society comedies are said to be plundered from Sardou and Dumas *fils*.

9

The extent to which Wilde's own voice emerges from this nineteenth-century chorus creates a difficult critical exercise. In some ways, it makes him an even more interesting, because so representative, writer. Wilde's breadth of reading, in classical as well as contemporary literature, and his propensity to absorb and reflect that reading, were not common among the late Victorians. The extent to which he seems to react to French literature, especially, helps to explain his relatively high reputation among foreign critics. This estimate in itself makes some English critics suspicious. Graham Hough, quoting with approval Wilde's description of Huysmans's style, and turning it on Wilde's own style to the latter's disadvantage, prefaces his comments with this disclaimer: 'Foreign judgements on these matters are generally unreliable, as Wilde's own reputation abroad can show us.'[22] Wilde's lack of insularity was expressed most intensely by his sympathy with French culture. His adoption of the French language for *Salomé*, a surprising anticipation of Beckett, marks the furthest stage of his literary exploration of others' voices.

Wilde's ability to mimic, to quote and to reflect is an additional reminder to avoid constructing too solemn or too constant a persona for the man as Artist. If one selects, for example, two famous contexts as poles, Wilde weeping before Keats's grave and Wilde the suffering Christ figure of Reading Gaol, too humourless a perspective may be constructed. Wilde wrote in absolutes, but also in paradoxes. He conceived of his vocation as the most crucial and central one that is offered, but he also preferred to exercise it modernly, wittily, elegantly and lightly. Something of those qualities are conveyed in the closing passages of 'The Critic as Artist':

GILBERT: Yes: I am a dreamer. For a dreamer is one who can only find his way by moonlight, and his punishment is that he sees the dawn before the rest of the world.
ERNEST: His punishment?
GILBERT: And his reward. But see, it is dawn already. Draw back the curtains and open the windows wide. How cool the morning air is! Piccadilly lies at our feet like a long riband of silver. A faint purple mist hangs over the Park, and the shadows of the white houses are purple. It is too late to sleep. Let us go down to Covent Garden and look at the roses. Come! I am tired of thought.[23]

Wilde's art, and his role as Artist, was itself conceived in the form of an extended dialogue, conducted within a variety of contexts, and in modulating and developing moods and tones. Lacking

10

Wilde's presence, his 'texture', one needs to search for the appropriate mood and tone of each work, remembering in the process Henry James's awful warning: 'Everything Oscar does is a deliberate trap for the literalist, and to see the literalist walk straight up to it, look straight at it, and step straight into it, makes one freshly avert a discouraged gaze from this unspeakable animal.'[24]

2

Oxford and the early poems

Wilde sailed for America on 24 December 1881 to undertake a lecture tour for the D'Oyly Carte management. The intention was
to display him as a living example of the aesthetic poets, Reginald
Bunthorne (the Fleshly variety) and Archibald Grosvenor (the
Idyllic), satirised in Gilbert and Sullivan's *Patience*, which had
opened in New York in September. One of the remarkable
features of this enterprise was the narrow base on which Wilde had
secured a reputation sufficient for the offer to have been contemplated. Wilde was twenty-seven. He had had a brilliant
university career as a classical scholar, first at Trinity College,
Dublin and then at Magdalen College, Oxford. In terms of
literary achievement, his output was confined to a collection of
poems which he had published at his own expense earlier in 1881,
and which were reviewed in generally unfavourable terms. A
number of these had been previously placed in periodicals, and he
had written three articles which appeared in Irish magazines. His
first play, *Vera, or The Nihilists*, had been privately printed and
distributed to a select circle: a production had been scheduled, but
cancelled because of political susceptibilities. However, Wilde's
gifts as wit and commentator, his studied self-image and careful
cultivation of the role of public entertainer, more than compen-
sated for the slenderness of his published work. The caricatures of
Wilde in *Punch* may be taken as an indication of his notoriety,
while Walter Hamilton devoted a substantial chapter to him in his
book *The Aesthetic Movement in England* which was published in
1882.

Wilde was born, on 16 October 1854, into a family accustomed,
one way and another, to being in the public eye. His father was
a notable Dublin medical man, an ear and eye surgeon, who was
appointed oculist to the Queen in Ireland and was knighted in
1864. Sir William Wilde was a versatile scholar and prolific
author, among whose interests were Celtic archaeology, natural
history, topography and Dean Swift. He was also a relentless
womaniser: one of his relationships involved him and his wife in
a scandalous law-suit. Lady Wilde, known by one of her *noms de*

plume, Speranza, was a great-niece of Charles Maturin, author of *Melmoth the Wanderer* and so literary godfather to Wilde, who took the name of Sebastian Melmoth during his last years of exile. She, too, was a spirited writer and poet, and an ardent Irish nationalist. She had achieved fame by rising to her feet in court during the prosecution of the editor of *The Nation* for sedition, and claiming authorship of an offending article which ran: 'Oh! for a hundred thousand muskets glittering brightly in the light of Heaven . . .' Among the French and German works she translated was a curious tale by Meinhold, *Sidonia the Sorceress*. She continued to write and to entertain regularly, though in a somewhat eccentric manner, in the Wildes' Merrion Square house. After her husband's death in 1876, she transferred herself and her *salon* to London. Speranza's literary tastes and interests – Keats and Shelley, Disraeli and Balzac – were passed on to her younger son. Oscar had an elder brother, Willie, and a younger sister, Isola, who died in 1867 at the age of eight, commemorated in Wilde's poem 'Requiescat'.

If Wilde's taste was partly moulded by his mother's Romanticism, his formal education, first at Portora Royal School and then at Dublin and Oxford, provided the classical counterbalance. So far as formal recognition was concerned, he acquired a most impressive collection of academic honours: gold medal, exhibition, a demyship at Magdalen, and the distinction of an Oxford double first. Subjectively, he accumulated a wide knowledge of classical thought and literature, which permeated his extremely retentive memory. Twice during the vacations he travelled through Italy, once, in the company of his Dublin tutor Mahaffy, through Greece. On each occasion, from the evidence of his letters and poems, it is clear how sharp an impact both countries made on his imagination, though Greece exercised the more potent and lasting influence. A fragment of a letter from Wilde to his mother reflects the delicate sense of tension between the Greek context and the romantic eye of the traveller:

The island is full of idyllic loveliness. Set in its olive woods. In Italy nearly all the olives are pollarded and stunted, but here one sees them in the fullness of their natural beauty.

What strikes one is extreme age, and the twisted broken writhing in pain such as Gustave Doré loves to draw. The delicate grey-green and silver of their leaves, changing to silver when the wind blows on them.[1]

Being in Greece meant infinitely more to Wilde than returning to Oxford to meet his academic commitments. As he wrote ingenuously to his Magdalen tutor, 'I hope you will not mind if I miss ten days at the beginning: seeing Greece is really a great education for anyone and will I think benefit me greatly, and Mr Mahaffy is such a clever man that it is quite as good as going to lectures to be in his society.'[2] The dons were not impressed; Wilde forfeited £47 10s., half the value of his demyship, and was sent down for the remainder of the term for being, as he put it, 'the first undergraduate to visit Olympia'.[3]

Mahaffy, it seems, was intentionally diverting Wilde from his primary destination of Rome, where he was intending, according to Mahaffy's companion George Macmillan, 'to see all the glories of the religion which seems to him the highest and the most sentimental'.[4] Although the fiercest controversies generated by the Oxford Movement had passed, Oxford in the 1870s offered the impressionable undergraduate an attractive experience of the Roman Catholic Church; the example of Newman still exercised a powerful influence. Some of Wilde's comments in his letters report his church-going and sermon-tasting in the same half-ironic, half-flippant tone he uses to record his lotus days of strawberry teas and tennis parties on country lawns. But a more serious vein is struck when he refers to Newman, whose life and writing he studied closely:

I now breakfast with Father Parkinson, go to St Aloysius, talk sentimental religion to Dunlop and altogether am caught in the fowler's snare, in the wiles of the Scarlet Woman – I may go over in the vac. I have dreams of a visit to Newman, of the holy sacrament in a new Church, and of a quiet and peace afterwards in my soul. I need not say, though, that I shift with every breath of thought and am weaker and more self-deceiving than ever.

If I *could hope* that the Church would wake in me some earnestness and purity I would go over *as a luxury*, if for no better reasons. But I can hardly hope it would, and to go over to Rome would be to sacrifice and give up my two great gods 'Money and Ambition'.

Still I get so wretched and low and troubled that in some desperate mood I will seek the shelter of a Church which simply enthrals me by its fascination.[5]

The fascination of the Roman Catholic Church was presented in a particularly vivid form to Wilde when he joined his Oxford friends William Ward and Hunter-Blair, the latter a recent convert to the Catholic faith, in Rome in the spring of 1877, on his return from Athens. Wilde soon found himself kneeling at an audience before Pope Pius IX, and receiving his blessing. The pagan and the Christian worlds had thus been placed before him in swift succession in their most intense form. One poem especially from this period seems to reflect Wilde's spiritual restlessness:

> Come down, O Christ, and help me! reach thy hand,
> For I am drowning in a stormier sea
> Than Simon on thy lake of Galilee:

though others, while clearly reflecting his experience of Italy and Rome, also indicate the extent of Wilde's reservations. For instance, Wilde places the splendour of 'The Holy Lord of Rome' –

> Priest-like, he wore a robe more white than foam
> And, king-like, swathed himself in royal red

in contrast

> To One who wandered by a lonely sea,
> And sought in vain for any place of rest.[6]

In the context of these religious yearnings, it is not surprising that Wilde embraced the cult of aestheticism with the fervour of an acolyte.

During his years at Oxford, Wilde came into personal contact with two men, Pater and Ruskin, whose ideas had a far-reaching influence upon him and upon his development as an artist. Walter Pater was a fellow of Brasenose College. It is not wholly certain when Wilde first met him. He sent Pater a copy of his review of the Grosvenor Gallery which appeared in the Dublin University magazine in July 1877, and in a letter to a friend quoted Pater's reply verbatim rather than trust so precious a document to the mercies of the postman:

Your excellent article on the Grosvenor Gallery I read with very great pleasure: it makes me much wish to make your acquaintance. and I hope you will give me an early call on your return to Oxford . . . The article shows that you possess some beautiful and, for your age, quite exceptionally cultivated tastes: and a considerable knowledge too of many beautiful things.

Wilde added, with a rare note of hesitancy: 'You won't think me snobbish for sending you this? After all, it *is* something to be honestly proud of.'[7]

In a later article, a review of Pater's book *Appreciations, with an Essay on Style*, Wilde recounted his first meeting with Pater. The

15

recollections are significant as comment on Wilde's perceptions of his Oxford period and serve, incidentally, as a criticism of his own work:

When I first had the privilege – and I count it a very high one – of meeting Mr Walter Pater, he said to me, smiling, 'Why do you always write poetry? Why do you not write prose? Prose is so much more difficult.'

It was during my undergraduate days at Oxford; days of lyrical ardour and of studious sonnet-writing; days when one loved the exquisite intricacy and musical repetitions of the ballade, and the villanelle with its linked long-drawn echoes and its curious completeness; days when one solemnly sought to discover the proper temper in which a triolet should be written; delightful days, in which, I am glad to say, there was far more rhyme than reason.

I may frankly confess now that at the time I did not quite comprehend what Mr Pater really meant; and it was not till I had carefully studied his beautiful and suggestive essays on the Renaissance that I fully realised what a wonderful self-conscious art the art of English prose-writing really is, or may be made to be.[8]

Equally significant is Wilde's admission that Pater's *Essays* became to him '"the golden book of spirit and sense, the holy writ of beauty". They are still this to me. It is possible, of course, that I may exaggerate about them. I certainly hope that I do; for where there is no exaggeration there is no love, and where there is no love there is no understanding.' Wilde's susceptibility to Pater's influence was maintained throughout his life. When in Reading Gaol he requested copies of Pater's *Gaston de Latour* and *Miscellaneous Essays*; and he wrote in *De Profundis*, 'I remember during my first term at Oxford reading in Pater's *Renaissance* – that book which has had such a strange influence over my life . . .'[9] Wilde was not given to admission of influence, as opposed to interest, but Pater he freely acknowledged: 'Setting aside the prose and poetry of Greek and Latin authors, the only writers who have influenced me are Keats, Flaubert, and Walter Pater; and' (he adds less convincingly) 'before I came across them I had already gone more than half-way to meet them.'[10] It is clear, too, that he found something impressive in Pater's life, though he would later mock him. Perhaps he saw in him someone who had mastered some of the conflicts he was conscious of within his own self and temperament: 'in Mr Pater, as in Cardinal Newman, we find the union of personality with perfection.'[11]

What did Pater's 'strange influence' on Wilde and on others consist of? Pater suppressed the conclusion to *The Renaissance* in its

16

second edition on the grounds that it 'might possibly mislead some of those young men into whose hands it might fall', implying that it was as dangerous to the impressionable as was the 'poison' book which Lord Henry Wotton gave to Dorian Gray. Pater's attitude is so tentative (the 'might possibly' is characteristic), his style so subtle and veiled, his own life so cautious, that it is difficult to appreciate the potential subversiveness of his thought. The particular nature of Pater's ideas may be sensed initially by way of contrast. Graham Hough, in *The Last Romantics*, made a clear and arresting distinction between the thrust of Pater's writing, if that is not too physical a word, and Arnold's:

Ethically Arnold is completely attached to the traditional moral scheme; emotionally he looks back with longing to the time when 'the sea of Faith too was at the full'. He intends to use the emotions associated with the greatest passages of the greatest literature as a perpetual monitor towards right action and right feeling; and he has not the slightest desire to alter the traditional conceptions of right action and right feeling.[12]

Arnold was part of the late-Victorian movement, which, faced with the destruction of received arguments, for instance about the authenticity of the scriptures as a basis for Christian belief, sought to replace them with subjective appeals to the promptings of the individual sensibility. Crudely, this may be categorised as a revisionist approach: the old order was right, but for the wrong reasons. The task of the modern philosopher was to adumbrate a new and convincing set of arguments for respecting the traditional moral and spiritual system.

Pater, though much of what he wrote could be used to further such an aim, is fundamentally opposed to Arnold's intention. 'Pater has none of Arnold's nostalgia for the age of faith; on the contrary, he quite complacently identifies himself with modernity; he has none of Arnold's longing for certitude; instead, he shows considerable willingness to involve himself in the flux.'[13] Discovery and experiment are the methods Pater advocates: his images of the world are those of deliquescence, instability, momentariness. The developmental replaces the absolute and the constant. This is the cast of mind which leads to Pater's promotion of the creed of individual feeling:

The service of philosophy, and of religion and speculative culture as well, to the human spirit, is to rouse, to startle it into a sharp and eager observation. Every moment some form grows perfect in hand or face; some tone on the hills or sea is choicer than the rest; some mood of passion or

17

insight or intellectual excitement is irresistibly real and attractive for us, – for that moment only. Not the fruit of experience, but experience itself is the end. A counted number of pulses only is given to us of a variegated, dramatic life. How may we see in them all that is to be seen in them by the finest senses? How can we pass most swiftly from point to point, and be present always at the focus where the greatest number of vital forces unite in their purest energy?

To burn always with this hard, gemlike flame, to maintain this ecstasy, is success in life . . . While all melts under our feet, we may well catch at any exquisite passion, or any contribution to knowledge that seems, by a lifted horizon, to set the spirit free for a moment, or any stirring of the senses, strange dyes, strange flowers, and curious odours, or work of the artist's hands, or the face of one's friend.[14]

As expressed here, it can be seen how ambivalent, or malleable, is Pater's philosophy. It requires interpretation, translation into practical terms, before it can be safely absorbed as a series of guiding principles. Pater provides a number of such interpretations in *Marius the Epicurean*: in fact, one might see the novel as a systematic response to the philosophical attitudes of Pater's earlier writings. The context of the following interpretation is a visit the young Marius makes to a temple of Aesculapius 'for the cure of some boyish sickness'. Marius falls asleep in the guest-chamber, in some dread of a night visitation from one of the sacred snakes kept in the palace. He wakes, after an hour's feverish dreaming, to find a priest sitting by his bedside, who puts forward the precept 'of a diligent promotion of the capacity of the eye, inasmuch as in the eye would lie for him the determining influence of life: he was of the number of those who, in the words of a poet who came long after, must be "made perfect by the love of visible beauty"'.

'If thou wouldst have all about thee like the colours of some fresh picture, in a clear light,' so the discourse recommenced after a pause, 'be temperate in thy religious motions, in love, in wine, in all things, and of a peaceful heart with thy fellows.' To keep the eye clear by a sort of exquisite personal alacrity and cleanliness, extending even to his dwelling place; to discriminate, ever more and more exactly, select form and colour in things from what was less select; to meditate much on beautiful objects, on objects, more especially, connected with the period of youth – on children at play in the morning, the trees in early spring, on young animals, on the fashions and amusements of young men; to keep ever by him if it were but a single choice flower, a graceful animal or sea-shell, as a token and representative of the whole kingdom of such things; to avoid jealousy, in his way through the world, everything repugnant to

18

sight; and, should any circumstance tempt him to a general converse in the range of such objects, to disentangle himself from that circumstance at any cost of place, money, or opportunity; such were, in brief outline, the duties recognised, the rights demanded, in this new formula of life.[15]

The discrimination of the eye, and the idea of the force for good derived from beautiful objects and surroundings, is apparent in much of Wilde's critical writing. (It is an idea derived also from Ruskin and Morris.) The horror of excess which Pater so clearly expressed here, as in his own life, was a matter of temperament as much as anything. An equally valid response to the dicta of *The Renaissance* would be to taste each experience that life afforded, a response which Wilde articulated through the persona of Lord Henry Wotton, as he sat talking to Dorian Gray in Basil Hallward's garden:

Live! Live the wonderful life that is in you! Let nothing be lost upon you. Be always searching for new sensations. Be afraid of nothing . . . a new Hedonism – that is what our century wants. You might be its visible symbol. With your personality there is nothing you could not do. The world belongs to you for a season . . .[16]

While Pater offered his subtle, cautious but potentially disruptive vision, and entertained selected undergraduates to tea in his beautifully furnished rooms, Ruskin, the Slade Professor of Art, gave his ideas a more robust and concrete form. Ruskin, through *Modern Painters, Seven Lamps of Architecture* and *The Stones of Venice*, did more than anyone to open the eyes of the Victorians to a new appreciation of visual art. He was the great theoretical precursor of the Pre-Raphaelites and of William Morris. Wilde's first encounter with him was in the Hinksey road-making project, a selective and lightly fictionalised account of which Wilde used in one of his American lectures. One summer afternoon Ruskin lectured to the undergraduates 'not on art this time but on life':

He thought, he said, that we should be working at something that would do good to other people, at something by which we might show that in all labour there was something noble. Well, we were a good deal moved, and said we would do anything he wished. So he went out round Oxford and found two villages, Upper and Lower Hinksey, and between them there lay a great swamp, so that the villagers could not pass from one to the other without many miles of a round. And when we came back in winter he asked us to help him to make a road across this morass for these village people to use. So out we went, day after day, and learned how to lay levels and to break stones, and to wheel barrows along a plank – a very difficult thing to do. And Ruskin worked with us in the mist and rain

19

and mud of an Oxford winter, and our friends and our enemies came out
and mocked us from the bank.

The road-building, and the road, collapsed; but Wilde used the
enterprise as a metaphor for the new movement at whose head he
appeared to see himself:

And I felt that if there was enough spirit amongst the young men to go
out to such work as road-making for the sake of a noble ideal of life, I
could from them create an artistic movement that might change, as it has
changed, the face of England.[17]

Ruskin's elevation of beauty was more systematic, more closely
argued, more energetically expressed than anything in Pater. His
feelings for the poor, for those who had suffered in both material
and spiritual terms from the depredations of the machine age of
the industrial revolution, and his wish to do something positive
and practical to restore dignity to labour, were instincts Wilde had
already imbibed from his mother. A later letter to Ruskin pays
tribute to the strength of his example:

the dearest memories of my Oxford days are my walks and talks with you,
and from you I learned nothing but what was good. How else could it be?
There is in you something of prophet, of priest, and of poet, and to you
the gods gave eloquence such as they have given to none other, so that
your message might come to us with the fire of passion, and the marvel
of music, making the deaf to hear, and the blind to see.[18]

The poet who absorbs the functions of prophet and priest is a
pointer to Wilde's understanding of the role of the artist.

The practical applications of Ruskin's principles were carried
out by the Pre-Raphaelites and by William Morris and his
followers. But the whole burden of Ruskin's teaching implied
change and improvement. His vision of the universe was, essentially, one of unity: unity between Nature (and so God) and man;
between Nature and art; between art and religion; and between
man and man. His mission was to overcome the Victorian
dullness of perception, to release and revitalise the senses, especially
the visual sense, and so free a sensibility that had become fettered
by habit, by the mechanical, by the divisiveness of social and
economic institutions. It often seems as if Ruskin wishes to
substitute the precept 'only see' for the traditional 'only believe'
– or, so close is the connection between the aesthetic and the
spiritual, 'only see and then believe'. The vigour with which he
conveys his own vision, the sharply articulated sense of what he

himself saw and experienced, is more compelling, perhaps, than his line of argument, impressively systematic though that is. But everywhere one is made conscious of the moral and social significance of his perceptions. There is no sense of a privileged aestheticism, such as one may acquire from Pater: of the careful cultivation of the individual life and sensibility. Ruskin sees each object as expressive of some other force or power, whether it is the lily carved on a capital, or St Mark's itself: the work of art is expressive of the imagination of the artist, but also of the age; the building is expressive of its architect and craftsmen, but also of the society it serves. These ideas are explored in *The Stones of Venice*, for example in the chapter 'The Nature of Gothic'. Ruskin is here contrasting the modern English room unfavourably with the Gothic cathedral:

And now, reader, look round this English room of yours, about which you have been proud so often, because the work of it was so good and strong, and the ornaments of it so finished. Examine again all those accurate mouldings, and perfect polishings, and unerring adjustments of the seasoned wood and tempered steel. Many a time you have exulted over them, and thought how great England was, because her slightest work was done so thoroughly. Alas! if read rightly, these perfectnesses are signs of a slavery in our England a thousand times more bitter and more degrading than that of the scourged African, or helot Greek. Men may be beaten, chained, tormented, yoked like cattle, slaughtered like summer flies, and yet remain in one sense, and the best sense, free. But to smother their souls within them, to blight and hew into rotting pollards the suckling branches of their human intelligence, to make the flesh and skin which, after the worm's work on it, is to see God, into leathern thongs to yoke machinery with, – this it is to be slave-masters indeed . . .

And on the other hand, go forth again to gaze upon the old cathedral front, where you have smiled so often at the fantastic ignorance of the old sculptors: examine once more those ugly goblins, and formless monsters, and stern statues, anatomiless and rigid; but do not mock at them, for they are signs of the life and liberty of every workman who struck the stone; a freedom of thought, and rank in scale of being, such as no laws, no charters, no charities can secure; but which it must be the first aim of all Europe at this day to regain for her children.[19]

Ruskin's thought, and his vision of art, is part of an essentially religious context, and one mediated through Christianity. The sense of a divine purpose behind all things marks the sharpest contrast with the invitation of Hedonism implied by Pater in *The Renaissance*, and with the earliest manifestations of Wilde's own attitudes.

Wilde acquired a reputation in London, once his university career was complete, through social rather than literary means. Sharing rooms with his Oxford friend, the artist Frank Miles, he pursued his vocation in a sphere wider than that offered by Oxford. With energy and discrimination, he cultivated the acquaintance of writers and artists, of actors and, more especially, actresses, of the beautiful and famous. His letters reflect the pleasure he found in such contacts: 'I am going tonight with *Ruskin* to see Irving as Shylock, and afterwards to the *Millais* Ball . . .';[20] 'I was very sorry you did not come to tea as I could have introduced you to some very beautiful people. Mrs Langtry and Lady Lonsdale and a lot of clever beings . . .';[21] 'Dear Mrs Hunt, Thank you so much for your kind invitations but I am in the "lion's den" on both days. Sunday I dine to meet Mr Lowell, a poet, statesman and an American in one! . . . And on Wednesday the 2nd I have a long-standing engagement to dine with Sir Charles Dilke . . .'[22] One tendency, significant in view of his future career as a dramatist, was the warmth of his friendships with actresses such as Ellen Terry, Helena Modjeska and Sarah Bernhardt. These friendships often had a professional dimension. Ellen Terry received a specially bound presentation copy of *Vera, or the Nihilists*, with an accompanying wish that some day Wilde might be 'fortunate enough to write something worthy'[23] of her playing. With Lily Langtry and Sarah Bernhardt, there was an additional public dimension. Wilde formed himself into a one-man reception committee for Sarah Bernhardt on her arrival at Folkestone and flung lilies at her feet. This talent for self-publicity, allied to his developing conversational brilliance and his cultivation of distinctive dress, rapidly promoted Wilde to the point where he became first a conversation piece and secondly, the national accolade, a subject for caricature. There were cartoons in *Punch*, such as George du Maurier's of the poet Jellaby Postlethwaite; there was the portrait of the aesthete Lambert Streyke in Burnand's play *The Colonel*; and, whether or not Gilbert had Wilde specifically in mind, the public certainly identified him with the languid poets of *Patience*. Remarkably, all these reflections of Wilde's image preceded the appearance of his first collection of verse in the summer of 1881.

Wilde paid all the expenses of *Poems*. Within a year five editions, of 250 copies each, had been published and largely sold, a result of Wilde's personal reputation rather than of the critical reception, which was largely dismissive. Reviewers delighted in cataloguing his dependence on Swinburne, Arnold, Rossetti, Tennyson and especially Keats. They accused him of insincerity and vacuity: 'The worst faults are artificiality and insincerity';[24] 'The author possesses cleverness, astonishing fluency, a rich and full vocabulary, and nothing to say . . . The book is not without traces of cleverness, but is marred everywhere by imitation, insincerity, and bad taste.'[25] In a much more perceptive notice Oscar Browning, admittedly a friend but vigorous in castigating what he held to be the poems' weaknesses, responded to the qualities of the writer: '. . . we lay down this book in the conviction that England is enriched with a new poet. If Mr Wilde, keeping his passion, his sense of beauty, his gifts of language and metre, will apply to himself the stern self-discipline through which alone those whom he admires have obtained the excellence which is theirs, there is no boyish dream of fame or ambition which he may not at some time satisfy.' Browning confessed himself to be bewildered 'by the irregular pulsations of a sympathy which never wearies. Roman Catholic ritual, stern Puritanism, parched Greek islands, cool English lanes and streams, Paganism and Christianity, despotism and Republicanism, Wordsworth, Milton, and Mr Swinburne, receive in turn the same passionate devotion.'[26] Browning's list of themes at least alerts us to the essential seriousness of the poems' content, though a glance through the titles of individual poems tends to confirm an impression of a miscellany of occasional pieces and literary responses: 'Sonnet on Approaching Italy'; 'Sonnet Written in Holy Week at Genoa'; 'Magdalen Walks'; 'Endymion'; 'The Grave of Shelley'.

Wilde has, however, imposed a structure on these poems. There is an opening key sonnet, 'Hélas', and a valedictory lyric, 'Flower of Love'; and the shorter poems are collected into sequences, each with a title: 'Eleutheria', 'Rosa Mystica', 'Wind Flowers', 'Flowers of Gold', 'Impressions de Théâtre', 'The Fourth Movement'. These sequences are interspersed, though not wholly systematically, with five much longer poems, all composed in the same metre: 'The Garden of Eros' follows 'Eleutheria'; 'The Burden of Itys', 'Rosa Mystica'; 'Charmides', 'Wind Flowers'; 'Panthea' precedes 'The Fourth Movement', and 'Humanitad' follows it.

The attempt at organisation, and the subject-matter of the poems, especially the five major pieces, constitute the most interesting element in the work. Individually, many of the poems are easy to disparage: derivative, facile, repetitive, mechanical, uneven. Cumulatively, one senses – more clearly in some places than others, it is true – that *Poems* represents a spiritual and imaginative odyssey and that the poetic voices Wilde assumes are in the nature of conscious experiments, necessary episodes in the exploratory journey that he had embarked upon. Far from concealing Wilde's literary and philosophical heritage, the poems specifically invoke his immediate referents (for instance, in 'The Garden of Eros', Keats, Byron, Morris, Rossetti, Burne-Jones), as well as his consciousness of various key figures and historical eras – Milton, Dante, Christ and, crucially, the Hellenic world. *Poems* also makes intermittent use of the idea of a physical journey based on Wilde's actual travels to Italy and Greece, a journey that is recollected and reflected upon in England. The first sequence, 'Eleutheria' (Freedom), contains a number of poems which lament England's and modern Europe's lost idealism. In 'Theoretikos, the Contemplative', the poet summarises the lapsed state of 'This mighty empire':

> Some enemy hath stolen its crown of bay,
> And from its hills that voice hath passed away
> Which spake of Freedom: O come out of it,
> Come out of it, my Soul, thou art not fit
> For this vile traffic-house, where day by day
> Wisdom and reverence are sold at mart . . .[27]

Instead, the poet advocates a position of withdrawn isolation, 'where in dreams of Art / And loftiest culture I would stand apart . . .' 'The Garden of Eros', in exploring the struggle for the artist to serve the Spirit of Beauty in the England of 'this scientific age', echoes the preceding sequence. The second sequence, 'Rosa Mystica', takes the poet-wanderer on to Italy, though to an Italy perceived as effectively in chains, and in the final line of 'Impression de Voyage' leaves him 'upon the soil of Greece at last'. The sense of physical place becomes less insistent, or less literal, from this point. Rather, the poet's modern English context is seen in tension with visions of Italy and Greece. 'The Burden of Itys' characterises 'This English Thames' as 'holier far than Rome', and the English fields are contrasted with Greek meadows. More significant, though, is the increasingly authoritative note of a new Hellenism that is sounded in 'Charmides', 'Panthea' and 'Humanitad', a belief, or set of beliefs and attitudes, that emerges as the artist's response to the dilemma posed in the epigraph. In 'Hélas', that dilemma is expressed in the form of a question, though one might be momentarily deceived into thinking that the first two lines articulate a late-Romantic ideal:

> To drift with every passion till my soul
> Is a stringed lute on which all winds can play,

until they are immediately countered by:

> Is it for this that I have given away
> Mine ancient wisdom, and austere control?[28]

The antithesis between the allure of passion, the 'honey of romance', and the austere demands of wisdom is one of a series that is developed, all to the disparagement of the modern age: the freedom of paganism is set against the restrictions of Christianity; the unified, pastoral world of ancient Greece against the divided, mercantile modern age. Common to them all is the implication that the artist is peculiarly isolated and vulnerable in the modern age, so that he both suffers from the acuteness of his perception and is compelled to assume the burden of formulating a response to the problem. Wilde, it must be admitted, is generally more successful in these poems in evoking a sense of the lost Golden Age and creating a pastoral idyll than in confronting and mastering the modern world.

In 'The Garden of Eros', the poet, a young Endymion, constructs an English summer pastoral landscape in an attempt to persuade the Spirit of Beauty to remain there, in spite of the 'new-found creeds' of 'this starved age':

> . . . tardy still, there are a few
> Who for thy sake would give their manlihood
> And consecrate their being, I at least
> Have done so . . .[29]

He then recalls the Spirit's other worshippers, beginning with Keats, the dominant source and influence of all these poems. But 'they are few'; 'all romance has flown', and 'this scientific age' has 'burst through our gates'. An 'age of Clay'

> Returns in horrid cycle, and the earth
> Hath borne again a noisy progeny
> Of ignorant Titans . . .[30]

The poem ends with the coming of day; but the sun, greeted with joy by the lark, is presented as an ambivalent God, linked to the testing function of the crucible of modern science:

> But the air freshens, let us go, why soon
> The Woodmen will be here; how we have lived this night of June![31]

25

Wilde brings *The Critic as Artist* to a close with a similar reference to the dawn. The implication seems to be that true life, artistic life, belongs to the moon and the night, while daybreak brings the woodmen.

'The Burden of Itys' develops several ideas from 'The Garden of Eros': the contrast between the Greek landscape (and Greek values and beliefs) and this 'English Thames' is maintained, but with the additional complexity of a corrupt Christianity as represented by Roman Catholicism:

> In a high litter red as blood and sin the Pope is borne[32]

and the evocation, by a song that inevitably must cease, of the old shapes of Beauty. This poem is transparently Wilde's ode to a nightingale, and the echoes and borrowings are open and frequent, as though Wilde is deliberately bringing to the reader's attention other exponents of pastoral, notably Spenser, Milton, Keats and Arnold, thus placing himself within a recognised tradition. At stanza 42, the reason why the poet is imploring the nightingale to sing on is made clear. The song cannot obliterate the image of

> The wan white face of that deserted Christ
> Whose bleeding hands my hands did once enfold . . .

A moment more, and

> Endymion would have passed across the mead
> Moonstruck with love . . .[33]

However, 'It was a dream, the glade is tenantless'; 'The Thames creeps on in sluggish leadenness'. The bird still sings, 'from Nuneham wood', but the landscape reverts to plain Oxfordshire,

> Warm valleys where the tired student lies
> With half-shut book, and many a winding walk
> Where rustic lovers stray at even in happy simple talk.

The poet, who has experienced the vision, is isolated from the pastoral calm, 'Drifting with every wind on the wide sea of misery', summoned back to Magdalen by the ominous last image:

Hark! 'tis the curfew booming from the bell at Christ Church gate.[34]

'Charmides' is the longest poem in the collection, consisting of 111 of the familiar stanzas. It contains a simple narrative in three phases, which correspond to the three sections of the poem. In the first, Charmides, a fisher-boy, journeys to Athena's temple,

26

conceals himself there, and throughout the night spends his passion on the goddess's statue; in revenge, the goddess appears to
him at sea, and Charmides leaps into the water to join his lover.
In the second, his body is cast up on shore, and a wood-nymph,
believing him to be only sleeping, lies down beside him and is
attempting to woo him when she is killed by an arrow from her
mistress Diana's bow. But her death-cries are heard by Aphrodite,
who prays to Proserpine to

> let Desire pass across dread Charon's icy ford.[35]

and in the brief third section, the lovers consummate their passion
in Acheron in 'one single ecstasy'.

The idea of Death-in-life and Life-in-death is a compelling one
for the late Romantics, and would be developed with much greater
skill and profundity by, especially, Yeats. Wilde's treatment
recalls William Morris in the *Earthly Paradise* tales, and the sensuous atmosphere may owe something to Rossetti, for instance in
the 'House of Life' sonnet sequence. That the poem's effect approaches the erotic was apparent to several reviewers, who quoted
with disapproval phrases such as 'the crescent thighs' or 'paddled
with the polished throat', or condemned the poem on the grounds
that it could not be recited in the presence of a lady. It certainly
contains an abundance of ornate language, and reveals Wilde's
attempt to create through style an artefact which reflects the
poem's central theme:

> And at our feet the water-snakes will curl
> In all their amethystine panoply
> Of diamonded mail, and we will mark
> The mullets swimming by the mast of some storm-foundered bark . . .[36]

Wilde is more successful in this decorated mode than in the evocation of physical passion, where his attempts to match the
Shakespeare of *Venus and Adonis* are more reminiscent of a Mills
and Boon novel:

> And longing arms around her neck he cast,
> And felt her throbbing bosom, and his breath came hot and fast . . .[37]

While the poem's atmosphere is arrestingly sensuous, its meaning
is not particularly clear. Charmides, named perhaps after
Socrates's pupil, experiences two contrasting acts of passion: one,
a violation of the temple and statue of the goddess of Wisdom, for
which the punishment is death; the other, a momentary ecstasy
contrived by Venus in the loveless land of Hades. Each act

27

represents the impulse towards unity and synthesis; each act is essentially self-destructive, doomed. The curfew of Christ Church bell is replaced in 'Charmides' by Persephone's summons to serve her 'by the ebon throne / Of the pale God'.[38]

In 'Panthea', the opposition of wisdom and feeling is restated in the opening stanzas, with the invitation to choose the latter:

> For, sweet, to feel is better than to know,
> And wisdom is a childless heritage,
> One pulse of passion – youth's first fiery glow, –
> Are worth the hoarded proverbs of the sage:
> Vex not thy soul with dead philosophy,
> Have we not lips to kiss with, hearts to love and eyes to see![39]

The call to Hedonism is a response to the bleak English landscape where the dreary north wind blows, a world from which God or the Gods have withdrawn, bequeathing a life blighted by a sense of guilt without even the hope of a twilight afterlife:

> No little coin of bronze can bring the soul
> Over Death's river to the sunless land,
> Victim and wine and vow are all in vain,
> The tomb is sealed; the soldiers watch; the dead rise not again.

Then, at its central hinge and verse, the poem reverses sharply in an affirmation of unity with nature:

> We are resolved into the supreme air,
> We are made one with what we touch and see . . .[40]

Here Wilde seems to offer an answer to the closed act of passion in 'Charmides', the form of words glancing at Pater and, perhaps, Wordsworth, in this Wildean ode on intimations of immortality:

> This hot hard flame with which our bodies burn
> Will make some meadow blaze with daffodil . . .

The rhetoric is more compelling than the argument; but the poem definitely moves towards a doctrine of individualism, in which the poet and his lover take their place as integral and active parts of the whole, not as merely detached observers:

> And we two lovers shall not sit afar,
> Critics of nature, but the joyous sea
> Shall be our raiment, and the bearded star
> Shoot arrows at our pleasure! We shall be
> Part of the mighty universal whole,
> And through all aeons mix and mingle with the Kosmic Soul!

We shall be notes in that great Symphony
Whose cadence circles through the rhythmic spheres,
And all the live World's throbbing heart shall be
One with our heart; the stealthy creeping years
Have lost their terrors now, we shall not die,
The Universe itself shall be our Immortality.[41]

'Humanitad', the last major poem in the collection, looks back
over the poet's spiritual odyssey. The first words, 'It is full winter
now: the trees are bare' are a response to the opening line of 'The
Garden of Eros', 'It is full summer now, the heart of June'. The
poet, the 'heir of pain', remains a seeker:

To burn with one clear flame, to stand erect
In natural honour, not to bend the knee
In profitless prostrations whose effect
Is by itself condemned, what alchemy
Can teach me this?[42]

He rejects Death, and Love, that 'noble madness', as solutions,
and, stranded beside the troubled waters, his Dover beach, passes
instead 'unto a life more barren, more austere', committing
himself to Athena. He finds it difficult, however, to turn his back
on the 'world's vain phantasies'; rather, his eyes 'restlessly follow'
that which from his 'cheated vision flies'. He seeks through
literature, history and art for 'one grand unselfish simple life / To
teach us what is wisdom!' Again, the yearning for unity emerges
as the central theme:

To make the Body and the Spirit one
With all right things, till no thing live in vain
From morn to noon, but in sweet unison
With every pulse of flesh and throb of brain
The soul in flawless essence high enthroned,
Against all outer vain attack invincibly bastioned . . .[43]

Such a perfect creed is denied modern man; and the restriction,
the chains under which the poet and all men chafe, is the doctrine
of self-denial, self-crucifixion, which is the legacy of Christianity:

But we have left those gentle haunts to pass
With weary feet to the new Calvary,
Where we behold, as one who in a glass
Sees his own face, self-slain Humanity,
And in the dumb reproach of that sad gaze
Learn what an awful phantom the red hand of man can raise.

29

OSCAR WILDE

O smitten mouth! O forehead crowned with thorn!
O chalice of all common miseries!
Thou for our sakes that loved thee not hast borne
An agony of endless centuries,
And we were vain and ignorant nor knew
That when we stabbed thy heart it was our own real hearts we slew.

The poem's final stanza proclaims man's capacity to come down
from the cross and be whole again:

Nay, nay, we are but crucified, and though
The bloody sweat falls from our brows like rain,
Loosen the nails – we shall come down I know,
Staunch the red wounds – we shall be whole again,
No need have we of hyssop-laden rod,
That which is purely human, that is Godlike, that is God.[44]

After this full-voiced affirmation, the envoi 'Flower of Love' is
surprisingly low-key. Rodney Shewan has pointed out that 'the
anti-climax is intentional since the lyric contains the poet's
apologia (the earliest expression of that attitude later to take the
epigrammatic form reported by Gide): "I have made my choice,
have lived my poems . . ." '[45] The antitheses explored in *Poems*
remained, not surprisingly, unresolved, resistant, perhaps, to
Wilde's command of poetic form and language. The collection,
nevertheless, did much to clarify Wilde's artistic purpose: nothing
less than a life's work.

3

Lectures and essays

Wilde arrived in New York on 2 January 1882, prepared in his role of Professor of Aesthetics to undertake the education of America. This was probably not the role envisaged by his sponsors (see p. 12 above), as intimated by Boucicault: 'Carte thought he had got hold of a popular fool. When he found that he was astride of a live animal instead of a wooden toy, he was taken aback.'[1] As usual with Wilde, it is difficult to tease out a consistent attitude. Letters to his friends recounting his triumphs swing between pride, relief and self-mockery: 'The hall had an audience larger and more wonderful than even Dickens had. I was recalled and applauded and am now treated like the Royal Boy';[2] 'I am torn in bits by Society. Immense receptions, wonderful dinners, crowds wait for my carriage. I wave a gloved hand and an ivory cane and they cheer.'[3] Once committed to the enterprise, Wilde determined that it should be an artistic, and financial, success. References to *Patience* were slight. In his chief lecture, published later as *The English Renaissance of Art*, he made only two allusions (though the 'aesthetic' dress he adopted for some of these lectures provided a different kind of reference point). The first, some two-thirds of the way through, subtly suggests that a New York audience badly needed a guide to Gilbert's satire: 'You have listened to *Patience* for a hundred nights and you have heard me only for one. It will make, no doubt, that satire more piquant by knowing something about the subject of it, but you must not judge of aestheticism by the satire of Mr Gilbert.'[4] The second, in his peroration, refers specifically to Bunthorne's song in Act One:

> Then a sentimental passion of a vegetable fashion must excite
>   your languid spleen,
> An attachment à la Plato for a bashful young potato, or a not-
>   too-French French bean!
> Though the Philistines may jostle you will rank as an apostle
>   in the high aesthetic band,
> If you walk down Piccadilly with a poppy or a lily in your
>   mediaeval hand.

Bunthorne's song is, in fact, confessional – 'a languid love for lilies' did not blight him:

> In short, my mediaevalism's affectation,
> Born of a morbid love of admiration!

Having established his general thesis in his lecture, Wilde risked a more sustained comparison:

You have heard . . . of two flowers connected with the aesthetic movement in England, and said (I assure you, erroneously) to be the food of some aesthetic young men. Well, let me tell you that the reason we love the lily and the sunflower, in spite of what Mr Gilbert may tell you, is not for any vegetable fashion at all. It is because these two lovely flowers are in England the two most perfect models of design, the most naturally adapted for decorative art . . .[5]

Wilde exploited the *Patience* connection with great skill. He instructed his manager, Colonel Morse, to order him two coats from a theatrical costumier's: 'They should be beautiful; tight velvet doublet, with large flowered sleeves of cambric coming up from under collar. I send you designs and measurements . . . They were dreadfully disappointed at Cincinatti at my not wearing knee-breeches.'[6] A few weeks earlier, at Boston, Harvard men had attempted to upstage him by attending his lecture dressed à la Bunthorne and carrying a lily or sunflower: Wilde out-manoeuvred them by wearing conventional evening dress, and using their appearance to establish a rapport with the audience. His was a carefully calculated set of performances, increasingly theatrical rather than educational, though his lecture technique was reportedly rather stilted and dull.

Wilde's repertory consisted at first of two principal lectures, 'The English Renaissance of Art' and 'Decorative Art in America'; later, in Chicago, he wrote 'The House Beautiful', and discarded 'The English Renaissance of Art', probably because it was too serious and theoretical. Later in the tour he also lectured on 'The Irish Poets of '48', a tribute to his mother. 'The English Renaissance' forms a continuum with the pattern of ideas laid out in *Poems*. As with the poems, he openly acknowledges the sources of his ideas; indeed, the sources form part of the argument, since he wishes to stress the essential and universal sense of unity which art can bestow, though he now widens his perspective to give proper consideration to such figures as Goethe and Gautier. Wilde's definition of the origin of the English Renaissance is presented in an early passage:

It is really from the union of Hellenism, in its breadth, its sanity of purpose, its calm possession of beauty, with the adventive, the intensified individualism, the passionate colour of the romantic spirit, that springs the art of the nineteenth century in England, as from the marriage of Faust and Helen of Troy sprang the beautiful boy Euphorion.[7]

Glancing at Pater, Wilde proceeds to gloss the difference between the classical and romantic spirit, between which

we may say that there lies this difference at least, that the one deals with the type and the other with the exception. In the work produced under the modern romantic spirit it is no longer the permanent, the essential truths of life that are treated of; it is the momentary situation of the one, the momentary aspect of the other that art seeks to render.[8]

Wilde now develops his concept of the English Renaissance as a 'passionate cult of pure beauty' with a 'flawless devotion to form'; and places at its centre the creative artist of whom Keats, 'pure and serene', is the perfect example and forerunner. The Pre-Raphaelite school, part of this great romantic movement, was primarily a return to Nature; and, in order to express properly this return, a redefinement of technique. Citing Baudelaire and Gautier, Wilde defines the absolute distinction of the artist not as 'his capacity to feel nature so much as his power of rendering it'. The vital controlling of the poet's imagination is extended to the choice of subject, and Wilde separates out, indeed elevates, a special realm for the artist, a 'consciousness of the absolute difference between the world of art and the world of real fact': 'Into the secure and sacred house of Beauty the true artist will admit nothing that is harsh or disturbing, nothing that gives pain, nothing that is debatable, nothing about which men argue.'[9]

Thus far, the aesthetic doctrine might be taken as broadly Paterian hedonism, the building up of a private and exquisite Palace of Art as a retreat from the ugliness and harshness of fact and reality. In the second half of the lecture, however, Wilde suggests that joy in art is a fundamentally social idea. While the creative artist is the high priest, child of his age but also spectator of all time and all existence, the critic (presumably here Wilde himself) has an important role, to 'create for art the social aim, too, by teaching the people the spirit in which they are to approach all artistic work, the love they are to give it, the lesson they are to draw from it'.[10]

Wilde, acknowledging the difficulty of bringing the Renaissance to fruition in England, because of the deadly influence of English commercial life, suggests that America 'might perfect this great movement of ours, for there is something Hellenic in your air and world'; only 'an increased sensibility to beauty' is lacking. As the lecture approaches its climax, the language becomes increasingly inspirational and religious in tone and reference: 'Love art for its own sake, and then all things that you need will be added to you'; the truths of art cannot be taught but only revealed, 'revealed to natures which have made themselves receptive to all beautiful impressions by the study and worship of all beautiful things'.[11] Wilde might be proclaiming the kingdom of heaven. He then becomes more pragmatic, emphasising the social value of surrounding oneself with delightful objects. These doctrines, however, form part of a gospel that is universal in its application. In a paragraph that reflects both Pater and Ruskin, Wilde also anticipates ideas which he will develop more potently in 'The Soul of Man under Socialism':

There are two kinds of men in the world, two great creeds, two different forms of natures; men to whom the end of life is action, and men to whom the end of life is thought. As regards the latter, who seek for experience itself and not for the fruits of experience, who must burn always with one of the passions of this fiery-coloured world, who find life interesting not for its secrets but for its situations, for its pulsations and not for its purpose; the passion for beauty engendered by the decorative arts will be to them more satisfying than any political or religious enthusiasm, any enthusiasm for humanity, any ecstasy or sorrow for love. For art comes to one professing primarily to give nothing but the highest quality to one's moments, and for those moments' sake. So far for those to whom the end of life is thought. As regards the others, who hold that life is inseparable from labour, to them should this movement be specially dear: for if our days are barren without industry, industry without art is barbarism.[12]

Wilde develops the need for joy and beauty in the life of the worker, in terms that rely heavily on the teaching of Morris and Ruskin. This is how the lily and the sunflower become relevant. 'There is nothing "in common life too mean, in common things to be ennobled by your touch"; nothing in life that art cannot sanctify'. Just as the lily and sunflower are in England 'perfect models of design', so, Wilde exhorts, 'let there be no flower in your meadows that does not wreathe its tendrils around your pillows, no little leaf in your Titan forests that does not lend its form to design'. Wilde thus brings his argument back to the primacy of nature, but also to the essential unity and unifying force of his modern romantic creed, ending, with an echo of the

Christian Gospel, with the aesthete's paradox, 'the secret of life is in art'.[13] It was a conclusion that he, at any rate, took seriously.

Wilde spent almost a year in the United States and Canada. His lecture programme, hectic to begin with, took him as far as Ottawa, San Francisco and New Orleans. When it dwindled, he remained in New York in an attempt to promote *Vera* (eventually performed there by Marie Prescott in August 1883) and to negotiate terms for *The Duchess of Padua* with Mary Anderson. On his return to Europe, he went first to London and then to Paris. There he lived off the proceeds of his lecture tour for three months or so, mixing with French writers and artists, and working on *The Duchess of Padua* and on his poem *The Sphinx*.

The American lectures seem very English in their cast of thought and phrase. Increasingly Wilde would use French culture and literature as a source of reference. During this initial visit he met Verlaine and Mallarmé, Zola and Edmond de Goncourt, Degas and Pissarro; and just as he had paid homage to the great literary figures of America, he was granted access to Victor Hugo. In his own rooms in the Hôtel Voltaire Wilde enacted a kind of imitation of Balzac. He announced that the 'Oscar of the first period' was dead; had his hair modelled after a bust of Nero in the Louvre; and carried an ivory cane of which the head was set with turquoises like Balzac's.

This sort of behaviour was harmless enough, though clearly puzzling to several of his French acquaintances, who did not always read the signs, or his wit, in the way that he intended. The recreation of a second Oscar was, nevertheless, a serious under-taking, a stage in the development of the cult of the dandy. In French literature, the key texts were Baudelaire's *Le Dandy*, and its immediate predecessor, Jules Barbey D'Aurevilly's *Du Dandysme*, which focusses upon Beau Brummell. The central idea is the fulfilment of the individual, within a hostile society, by his eleva-tion to the status of a thing, an elevation in which his perfect exterior becomes symbolic of his true value. Such an idea can be traced through Wilde's later work, in such manifestations as Lord Henry Wotton's definition of Dorian Gray as a perfect type, or in the dandies of the social comedies, Lord Darlington, Lord Illingworth and, supremely, Lord Goring. In contemporary French literature, the most vivid example was to be Huysmans's creation of Des Esseintes in *A Rebours*, a decadent variation modelled upon Count Robert de Montesquiou. The idea's ultimate projection in Wilde comes in his statement in *De Profundis*: 'I was a man who stood in symbolic relations to the art and culture of my age.'[14]

The search for perfection of style in the individual, which reaches a decadent absurdity in excessive attention to the trivia of appearance, is a product of the search for perfection of style in art. Here, for Wilde, as for so many affected by the Art for Art's sake doctrine, the key figure was Gautier. The Preface to Gautier's novel *Mademoiselle de Maupin* contained ideas which Wilde reformulated, but scarcely advanced beyond:

Les choses sont belles en proportion inverse de leur utilité. Il n'y a de vraiment beau que ce qui ne peut servir à rien. Tout ce qui est utile est laid.[15]

Gautier prefigured Wilde, too, in his rejection of Christianity because of the sense of shame it had imposed on mankind. From him, either directly or through the reflections of Gautier's successors – Flaubert, Baudelaire, Pater – Wilde absorbed the idea of the primacy of art, and the artist's sacred obligation to achieve mastery of his craft and materials. From him, especially, he acquired the impulse to make language function in the same way as pigment and stone. In *De Profundis*, he reiterates that, like Gautier, he is a man 'pour qui le monde visible existe'. In *Emaux et Camées*, Gautier's 1852 collection, comes the classic exposition in the poem 'L'Art':

> Fais les sirènes bleues,
> Tordant de cent facons
> Leurs queues,
> Les monstres des blasons;
>
> Tout passe. – L'art robuste
> Seul a l'éternité:
> Le buste
> Survit à la cité.
>
> Sculpte, lime, cisèle;
> Que ton rêve flottant
> Se scelle
> Dans le bloc résistant![16]

Reaction to Gautier's blue sirens writhing their tails may have been responsible for Wilde's over-indulgence in word-pictures, most noticeably in his stories. His general concept of art and the status of the artist, however, seems in its later expression to be fundamentally in tune with Gautier's evocation of 'L'art robuste'.

If Gautier was the original source, and an inspiring model in his later explorations of the medium of theatre in his ballet scenarios, more immediate influences were Wilde's acknowledged masters, Baudelaire and Flaubert. Baudelaire's attitudes, especially his elevation of the artist over nature, were transmitted in England partly through Whistler, who preceded Wilde in his absorption of French culture and ideas. Wilde's own critical essays are full of echoes, even paraphrases, from Baudelaire. Baudelaire's extension of the search for beauty to the dark side of experience, especially to the vicious, urban underworld, provided Wilde with a compelling precedent.

In prose style, and perhaps in his realisation of the role of artist, Flaubert was and remained Wilde's master. The inseparability of form and idea, the search for stylistic perfection in the expression of a thought, the total harmony and inter-relationship of every part within the work, were ideals with which Wilde was wholly in sympathy, even if he seldom approached Flaubert's purity of style. Flaubert's achievement in filtering out the author's subjective emotions was an attitude Wilde might admire, but could not emulate. The preface to *The Picture of Dorian Gray* is indebted to Flaubert; but the dictum 'To reveal art and to conceal the artist is art's aim' is not finally reconcilable with Wilde's more public interpretation of the role of artist.

From Paris Wilde made a brief visit to New York to see the production of *Vera*, which ran for only a week. He then returned to London, and by November was engaged to Constance Lloyd, whom he married on 29 May 1884. Although any pleasure in lecturing had long since been dissipated, Wilde found it a convenient way to earn money, being now able to add 'Impressions of America' to the familiar message of 'The House Beautiful'. Marriage, the furnishing of his own house beautiful at 16, Tite Street, and the birth of his two sons Cyril and Vyvyan, imposed considerable financial pressure. This he met by accepting a wide range of journalistic work, including reviewing, and, for two years, the editorship of the *Woman's World*. His ephemeral criticism still reads freshly. The more substantial essays he revised and collected in the volume *Intentions*, published in 1891, and these four essays, together with 'The Soul of Man under Socialism', comprise a systematic development of the concepts of critic and artist already suggested in 'The English Renaissance'.

The four essays of *Intentions* are 'The Decay of Lying', a revision of an essay first published in *Nineteenth Century*; 'Pen, Pencil, and

Poison', reprinted from *Fortnightly Review*, 1889; 'The Critic as
Artist', a revised form of 'The True Function and Value of
Criticism', from *Nineteenth Century*, 1890; and 'The Truth of
Masks', which first appeared in a slightly different form as
'Shakespeare and Stage Costume', again in *Nineteenth Century*,
1885.

The most objective essay is 'The Truth of Masks'. While it is
of considerable interest, both in terms of developing attitudes to
mise-en-scène and as a prelude to Wilde's own mastery of the visual
dimension in his plays, it is not particularly original. Most of the
ideas and many of the factual details with which the essay, rather
uncharacteristically, is stuffed, can be traced to E. W. Godwin's
essays on the architecture and costume of Shakespeare's plays,
first published in *The Architect* in 1875, and later reprinted by
Gordon Craig in *The Mask*. Godwin was designing the décor for
Wilde's house in Tite Street at the time Wilde was preparing his
essay. Wilde first addressed the question of the visual dimension
in Shakespeare's plays in an article for the *Dramatic Review* (14
March 1885), 'Shakespeare on Scenery', where he argued that
Shakespeare would have approved of the scenic innovations of the
modern stage. Wilde developed the argument at greater length in
'Shakespeare and Stage Costume', which purports to be a reply
to an article by Lord Lytton attacking 'archaeology' in stage
design, though in fact Lytton's piece is a review of Mary Anderson as Juliet, and the passing stricture on archaeology occurs in
a footnote.

Wilde's essay refers to a number of productions, most reson-
antly to the open-air performance of *As You Like It* directed by
Godwin and Lady Archibald Campbell at Coombe House. In this
production Lady Archibald Campbell played Orlando, an andro-
gynous experiment which recalled for Wilde Gautier's
Mademoiselle de Maupin, and the episode in which Maupin, in the
male disguise of Theódore de Sérannes, plays Rosalind. As
Shewan comments, Lady Archie's performance 'must have been
one of the principal stimuli for Wilde's two imaginative projec-
tions of idealised Shakespearean actors: she is the progenitor not
merely of Sibyl Vane but also of Willie Hughes'.[17]

The appropriate décor and costume for Shakespeare's plays was
still a current issue for Irving's theatre, though it had been within
the range of English critical attention since J. R. Planché's
archaeologically accurate costume designs for Charles Kemble,
and became prominent again during Macready's tenure of Covent

Garden and Drury Lane, and in connection with the productions of Charles Kean. Wilde assembles an impressive amount of evidence to emphasise the importance Shakespeare placed on the visual element not simply as a means of 'adding picturesqueness to poetry', but to demonstrate 'that he saw how important costume is as a means of providing certain dramatic effects',[18] and as a mode of intensifying dramatic situation. This kind of commentary, which recognises the function of effects as various as the processions in *Henry VIII*, the transformation of Prospero into the Duke of Milan, and the holes in Launce's boots, was relatively commonplace as criticism, even if rarely pursued with as much sensitivity and discrimination. Wilde, however, perceives the implications for practical stagecraft, recognising the need to respond to the truth of a play, rather than, pedantically, to the facts, and, more radically, that the vision of that truth should be the responsibility of one individual: 'one single mind directing the whole production. The facts of Art are diverse, but the essence of artistic effect is unity.'[19] Here Wilde writes in much the same terms as Gordon Craig would later develop more stringently in *The Art of the Theatre*, putting forward a doctrine that is a truism today but was very far from being realised even in the productions of Henry Irving. The essay ends on a warning note which takes the reader back to the title. Wilde was unlikely to countenance anything which smacked of realism. The archaeological impulse, he argued, was a movement which did not aim to reproduce life, but rather had 'the illusion of truth for its method, and the illusion of beauty for its result'.[20] The true drama possessed, for Wilde, the special facility of presenting life under the conditions of art.

The essay, elevated from the workmanlike 'Shakespeare and Stage Costume' into something more resonant by its new title, 'The Truth of Masks, a Note on Illusion', is more impressive as an indication of Wilde's theatrical instincts than as an exploration of critical theory. Wilde supplied with it a typically offhand disclaimer:

Not that I agree with everything that I have said in this essay. There is much with which I entirely disagree . . . For in Art there is no such thing as universal truth.[21]

The postscript signals, perhaps, Wilde's recognition that his expression was insufficiently enigmatic and paradoxical. When giving permission for a French translation of *Intentions*, he asked the translator to ignore 'The Truth of Masks' – 'je ne l'aime

OSCAR WILDE

plus' – and to substitute 'The Soul of Man under Socialism', 'qui contient une partie de mon esthétique'.[22]

'Pen, Pencil, and Poison, A Study in Green', is an essay on Thomas Griffiths Wainewright. It is written in Wilde's most disarmingly shocking manner: having listed the attributes of his subject as a man of artistic temperament – poet, painter, art critic, antiquarian – he adds as climax, after a preparatory flourish has praised Wainewright as 'a forger of no mean or ordinary capabilities', the final qualification, 'a subtle and secret poisoner almost without rival in this or any age'.[23]

The study, a kind of imaginary portrait, takes Wilde's interest in the idea of the mask one stage further than in the essay on Shakespeare. Wainewright at times seems to be serving as a substitute for Wilde himself. For example, he writes 'a series of articles on artistic subjects', but under a number of fanciful pseudonyms, grotesque masks 'under which he chose to hide his seriousness, or to reveal his levity', for 'A mask tells us more than a face'. Like Disraeli, or Wilde himself, Wainewright 'determined to startle the town as a dandy, and his beautiful rings, his antique cameo breast-pin, and his pale lemon-coloured kid gloves . . . were regarded by Hazlitt as being the signs of a new manner in literature'.[24] This is the kind of apparently flippant comment which Wilde intends to be taken seriously as well as to irritate: it is echoed by Lord Henry Wotton describing Dorian Gray, and by Wilde's description of Lord Goring. Wainewright moved through literary society, concealing his terrible sin like Dorian Gray; and his tastes and interests – like Gautier, and Wilde, he was fascinated by the Sphinx, that 'sweet marble monster' of both sexes – prefigure those of Dorian Gray, or reflect those of Wilde himself.

As the study proceeds, through a sequence of not especially convincing quotations from Wainewright's art criticism, one becomes increasingly less conscious of Wainewright himself, and more alert to the features which Wilde chooses to draw to our attention. As with Pater's portrait of Marius, it becomes clear that, through the mask of Wainewright, Wilde is displaying facets of his own personality. One relatively inconsequential example of this is a comment such as: 'Like most artificial people, he had a great love of nature.'[25] As the essay proceeds to its conclusion, however, the parallels become more disturbing, especially since Wilde's flippancy is most prominent in his handling of Wainewright's crimes. The references to bankruptcy proceedings, trials and transportation

become heavily ironic in the light of Wilde's future; while his comment that 'one can fancy an intense personality being created out of
sin',[26] with its suggestion that any action may be justified if it leads
to a development in style, imply the artist's ultimate challenge to
society. The context for Wilde's observation was an oil-portrait
apparently painted by Wainewright after his transportation to
Hobart; it was said that Wainewright 'had contrived to put the
expression of his wickedness into the portrait of a nice, kind-hearted
girl'. The idea of the criminal artist and the motif of the corrupted
picture form an interesting prelude to the career of Dorian Gray.

'The Truth of Masks' and 'Pen, Pencil, and Poison', for all
their insights and illuminations, still seem exercises in occasional
criticism, glittering yet isolated. 'The Decay of Lying', whose
dialogue form increases the potential for self-discrimination, at
once makes stronger claims on the attention. Wilde chooses names
for his conversationalists (Cyril and Vivian, his own children's
names), a setting, the library of a country house in Notting-
hamshire, a time, late afternoon, even an entrance for Cyril –
'coming in through the open window from the terrace'.[27] Cyril,
ostensibly, is the innocent inquirer and proponent of the natural
– 'Let us go and lie on the grass, and smoke cigarettes, and enjoy
Nature' – in contrast to Vivian, the intellectual, who has been
cooped up all day in the library writing an article entitled 'The
Decay of Lying: A Protest'. Wilde's method is for Vivian to read
the piece to Cyril, to whose occasional comments and questions
Vivian responds in a less formal mode. The whole is firmly held
within a sense of the appropriate length of time for such discussion. Having dismissed the claims of Nature as a source of
imagination and proved, to his own satisfaction, that 'external
Nature also imitates Art', and is thus subservient, Vivian suggests
that they leave the library for the terrace:

At twilight nature becomes a wonderfully suggestive effect, and is not
without loveliness, though perhaps its chief use is to illustrate quotations
from the poets. Come! We have talked long enough.[28]

The quotations nature calls to mind are from Tennyson and, with
calculated self-reference, Wilde himself.

The modern Socratic dialogue is a highly suitable form for
Wilde. It enables him to be both fanciful and serious: 'underneath
the fanciful form it hides some truths, or perhaps some half-truths,
about art, which I think require to be put forward'.[29] In *De Profundis*, Wilde refers to what is probably the genesis of the essay:

41

One of the most delightful dinners I remember ever having had is one Robbie and I had together in a little Soho cafe, which cost about as many shillings as my dinners to you used to cost pounds. Out of my dinner with Robbie came the first and best of all my dialogues. Idea, title, treatment, mode, everything was struck out at a 3 franc 50 c. *table-d'hôte.*[30]

Behind the polish of Wilde's cadences, the spontaneity of his conversation can still be discerned.

'The Decay of Lying' is a contribution to the contemporary debate about realism, specifically in art, in fiction and in drama, an attack on 'the monstrous worship of facts' of which Zola and Mrs Humphry Ward are selected as examples, and on modernity of form as well as modernity of subject-matter. The double structure – the enveloping dialogue, and the extracts from Vivian's essay which it contains – permits Wilde to be smartly contemporary in manner, to refer to society, the Church, education, politics, the law, journalism, and at the same time to set out the doctrines of his new aesthetics. These he conveniently summarises at the close: first, 'Art never expresses anything but itself'; secondly, 'All bad art comes from returning to Life and Nature, and elevating them into ideals'; thirdly, 'Life imitates Art far more than Art imitates Life'; while the final revelation is 'that Lying, the telling of beautiful untrue things, is the proper aim of Art'.[31]

Wilde lends his theory a certain panache by enlisting a number of artists to serve as examples on either side – Balzac, good, Zola, bad – and even if he never specifies what in their work actually validates or condemns it, they give a substance to his argument, or rather to his creed. Besides, the informality of the dialogue invites the expression of opinion, rather than excessive justification. Where the essay is less successful is in the 'poetic' elaborations of the potency of Art:

She can bid the almond-tree blossom in winter, and send the snow upon the ripe cornfield. At her word the frost lays its silver finger on the burning mouth of June, and the winged lions creep out from the hollows of the Lydian hills.[32]

To this evocation, Cyril responds: 'I like that. I can see it.' Wilde undercuts Cyril's innocent approval by having him add 'Is that the end?', to which Vivian's laconic reply promises practical methods 'by which we could revive this lost art of lying'; but it is still hard to escape the conclusion that Wilde intends his poetically charged prose flourish to serve as an analogy to the Oriental, self-delighting and self-justifying art he wishes to champion.

Wilde's critic, indeed, sees himself essentially as an artist, even if the Wildean doctrines are not yet perfectly and wholly formulated. At one point Vivian appears, by his insistence on the idea of the mask, to be arguing himself into a dismissal of individuality:

It is a humiliating confession, but we are all of us made out of the same stuff . . . Where we differ from each other is purely in accidentals: in dress, manner, tone of voice, religious opinions, personal appearance, tricks of habit and the like.[33]

Vivian conveniently breaks off his recital at this juncture. Wilde seems primarily to be exploring his own relationship with his public: the artistic critic who goes into society to delight the dinner-table, or to admire, at the request of a Mrs Arundel, 'one of those absurdly pretty Philistines', a sunset which is 'simply a very second-rate Turner, a Turner of a bad period'; but who also sits in his library correcting proofs of an essay on the doctrines of the new aesthetics. That essay's final revelation, that 'Lying, the telling of beautiful untrue things, is the proper aim of Art', represents the carefully constructed mask of the author himself.

Both the two parts, or acts, and the dialogue form of 'The Critic as Artist' give it a dramatic flavour, an effect enhanced by some surface similarities with *The Importance of Being Earnest* – not just the name of Ernest, but the essay's opening image of Gilbert at the piano, the interruption of the discussion for refreshment in the shape of Chambertin and ortolans, and the tone of the more frivolous exchanges, which is, of course, the tone of Wilde himself, the urbane conversationalist. The serious approach to aesthetics which makes up the content of the dialogue is deliberately clothed in an elegant form which is intended to entertain as much as to inform, and to give the impression that the conducting of an aesthetic argument is itself an art that demands a high level of sensitivity as to the appropriate time, setting and duration.

The first part, or act, is concerned with the emergence of a definition of criticism, and the role of the critic; this is developed through Gilbert, in response to Ernest's plea for the artist to be left alone and his claim that 'in the best days of art there were no art-critics'.[34] Gilbert asserts first, that the Greeks were a nation of art critics; that the Greeks regarded the medium of language, especially oral language, as superior to painting or sculpture; that there is no opposition between the creative and critical faculties, since all imaginative work is self-conscious and self-consciousness and the critical spirit are one; that creativity and criticism go together, since it is the critical faculty that invents fresh forms; that criticism demands more cultivation than creation; that the critic, in short, is an artist. Criticism, the record of one's soul, is 'the purest form of personal impression':[35] in this definition, a work of art is taken as a starting point for what amounts to a new creation which supersedes the original. These new literary creations constitute a kind of apex, for all other arts can be transformed into literature, so that Ruskin's response to Turner or Pater's to Leonardo da Vinci are new works of art, superior (it is implied) to the work which forms their ostensible subject.

The second phase of 'The Critic as Artist' widens the scope of discussion, and increases the claims and sphere of the critic–artist. First, Wilde asserts the primacy of Art over Life and of thought over action. Whereas Life is 'terribly deficient in form'[36] and incapable of repeating an emotion, Art offers every conceivable mood or passion within perfection of form. Similarly, the task of man does not lie with the ethical, practical world of action but with the dangerous, immoral sphere of Art, where the individual soul is perfected through contemplation: contemplation is 'the proper occupation of man'.[37] Wilde, somewhat belying his public persona though reflecting the extent of his own scholastic capacity, outlines a formidable programme for the true critic. 'To realize the nineteenth century, one must realize every century that has preceded it and that has contributed to its making. To know anything about oneself, one must know all about others. There must be no mood with which one cannot sympathize, no dead mode of life that one cannot make alive.'[38] This is the ideal of the chameleon poet, but Wilde here restricts him to 'dead' modes of life, as opposed to the explorations into 'Life' of Dorian Gray. The idea of sympathy, too, will recur, in Wilde's interpretation of Christ in *De Profundis*.

Having established the truth of the creativity of the critic, Wilde then confronts the objection that such work must of necessity be purely subjective. Wilde, through Gilbert, has a number of answers, not all equally convincing. One is the unsupported assertion that artists reproduce themselves, whereas criticism is always moving on. (This seems rather risky ground for Wilde to venture upon.) Another takes the shape of examples of the variety of objective critical forms, such as, inevitably, the dialogue, or the narration of Pater. At this point the external features of Wilde's own dialogue become more evident:

44

ERNEST: By its means, too, he can invent an imaginary antagonist, and convert him when he chooses by some absurdly sophisticated argument.

GILBERT: Ah! it is so easy to convert others. It is so difficult to convert oneself. To arrive at what one really believes, one must speak through lips different from one's own.[39]

The idea of the mask is infinitely malleable. It allows Wilde to refute three conventional attributes of the true critic, which Ernest naively and conveniently proposes: the qualities of fairness, rationality and sincerity. In their place, Gilbert advances temperament, a 'temperament exquisitely susceptible to beauty, and to the various impressions that beauty gives us',[40] a concept reminiscent of Pater. He proceeds to delineate the necessary environment for such a temperament, an environment in which the decorative arts, with their emphasis on form, predominate: 'it is Form that creates not merely the critical temperament, but also the aesthetic instinct . . .'[41] Ernest still clings to the old-fashioned notion that the critic might have some kind of effect on the artist. But the true critic, Gilbert replies, is a self-delighting concept. The critic 'will represent the flawless type. In him the culture of the century will see itself realized. You must not ask of him to have any other aim than the perfecting of himself.'[42]

As the dialogue nears its end, the claims of the critic become increasingly immodest. The critic speaks to the age, not to the individual; looks to the future, not the present; is more capable of judgment than the artist, since he is not blinded by the energy of creation; possesses the wide vision of contemplation, rather than the confined vision of creation. (Wilde seems to overlook here Gilbert's earlier claims for the primacy of the creative power of the critic.) Finally, Gilbert enlists some powerful allies in his cause:

You have spoken against Criticism as being a sterile thing. The nineteenth century is a turning-point in history, simply on account of the work of two men, Darwin and Renan, the one the critic of the Book of Nature, the other the critic of the books of God. Not to recognize this is to miss the meaning of one of the most important eras in the progress of the world. Creation is always behind the age. It is Criticism that leads us. The Critical Spirit and the World Spirit are one.

Ernest introduces a note of irony in his next question:

And he who is in possession of this spirit, or whom their spirit possesses, will, I suppose, do nothing?

Gilbert's answer describes the apotheosis of the critic:

He will look out upon the world and know its secret. By contact with divine things he will become divine. His will be the perfect life, and his only.[43]

Ernest's summary of what he has been told ends with a note of pity: 'My friend, you are a dreamer', a title that Gilbert accepts, along with the paradoxical punishment and reward 'that he sees the dawn before the rest of the world'. It is characteristic of the individualism, or uniqueness, of Wilde's concept of the critic as artist, that he contrives to evoke a Christ-like figure of suffering insight, before the vision fades in the impressionism of a London dawn:

It is too late to sleep. Let us go down to Covent Garden and look at the roses. Come! I am tired of thought.[44]

'The Soul of Man under Socialism' takes up the conflict already set out in 'The Critic as Artist' between individualism and altruism. Wilde argues that altruism, the 'sordid necessity of living for others', is unhealthy, since it prolongs the evils it professes to cure. Under present conditions, only an exceptional man (Wilde instances Darwin, Keats, Renan, Flaubert) is able to isolate himself and so 'realise the perfection that is in him'. Socialism, by freeing men from the necessity of living for others, would enable each man to fulfil his individuality.

Wilde's ideal society, which he recognises as Utopian – 'A map of the world that does not include Utopia is not worth even glancing at, for it leaves out the one country at which Humanity is always landing'[45] – strikes a modern note now, with its implicit programme to revolutionise rather than reform society, to abolish private property, and to free man from undignified labour by the development of machinery. How this is to be brought about involves a detail with which Wilde seldom concerned himself, though the means must not be authoritarian socialism, for 'Authority of all kinds, even democratic government is degrading.' Instead, 'The State is to be a voluntary association that will organise labour, and be the manufacturer and distributor of necessary commodities. The State is to make what is useful. The individual is to make what is beautiful.' The individual, under this system, is also to be 'left quite free to choose his own work'. This may be wishful thinking, but it leaves Wilde free to develop both his critique of present society and, more dynamically, his concept of the individual.

Wilde, though he shared his mother's concern for the poor and the outcast, cannot sustain his interest in them (as opposed to the criminal) for very long, though the passages in which he describes their predicament are among the most incisive in the essay:

Man should not be ready to show that he can live like a badly fed animal. He should decline to live like that, and should either steal or go on the rates, which is considered by many to be a form of stealing. As for begging, it is safer to beg than to take, but it is finer to take than to beg. No: a poor man who is ungrateful, unthrifty, discontented, and rebellious, is probably a real personality, and has much in him.[46]

This admiration for what would conventionally be regarded as anti-social behaviour develops by reference to the teaching of Jesus. In a section crucial to the essay's argument, Wilde states that 'the message of Christ to man was simply "Be thyself." '[47] Wilde achieves this interpretation by omitting all reference to the Kingdom of God, and substituting the human personality, in a manner that has been made familiar by twentieth-century theologians:

What Jesus means was this. He said to man, 'You have a wonderful personality. Develop it. Be yourself. Don't imagine that your perfection lies in accumulating or possessing external things. Your perfection is inside of you.'

From this, Wilde is able to assert that 'he who would lead a Christlike life is he who is perfectly and absolutely himself' – poet, scientist, student, shepherd, child, fisherman, or, significantly, criminal: a man 'may commit a sin against society, and yet realize through that sin his true perfection'.[48]

In passages of the essay which are less arresting (only because more familiar from his previous work), Wilde pursues the topic of the creative individualism of the artist, and the authority of the public, especially as exercised by its chosen instrument of torture, the press. Wilde rides several of his hobby-horses: he contrasts England with France to the disadvantage of the former, and plays with some cant terms of criticism aimed at the exponents of aestheticism, such as 'immoral', 'morbid' and 'unhealthy'. The essay, however, abandons this aside and returns to the major issue, the development of individualism. Wilde needs to defend his idea from the accusation of egotism. He does this by arguing that 'Selfishness is not living as one wishes to live, it is asking others to live as one wishes to live. And unselfishness is letting other people's lives alone, not interfering with them.'[49] Man must develop beyond the understandable but essentially limiting sympathy that responds to suffering; this, Wilde states with appropriate irony, is the 'least fine' mode of sympathy: 'It is tainted with egotism. It is apt to become morbid.' Instead, man should sympathise with 'life's joy and beauty and energy and health and freedom'. The final paragraphs outline a new doctrine to supersede that of Christ, whose medieval individualism could only be realised through pain or in solitude. Wilde's Renaissance individualism is ultimately social, to be realised through pleasure and the joy of living:

The new Individualism, for whose service Socialism, whether it wills it or not, is working, will be perfect harmony. It will be what the Greeks sought for, but could not, except in Thought, realize completely because they had slaves, and fed them; it will be what the Renaissance sought for, but could not realise completely except in Art, because they had slaves, and starved them. It will be complete, and through it each man will attain to his perfection. The new Individualism is the new Hellenism.[50]

The essay represents Wilde at his most original. It is comparatively easy to raise objections to his argument: his use of Christ's teaching, for instance, is highly selective and specious. Yet the essay is full of individual, thought-provoking insights, and the general thrust of its critique of late-Victorian society and modes of thinking is of more than historical interest. The style is more direct and combative than the highly polished and at times slightly precious elegance of the dialogues. If the authorial voice emerges from behind a mask, it is a mask which Wilde may not have wished to discard lightly. As he reflected later in *De Profundis*,

I see a far more intimate and immediate connection between the true life of Christ and the true life of the artist, and I take a keen pleasure in the reflection that long before Sorrow had made my days her own and bound me to her wheel I had written in *The Soul of Man* that he who would lead a Christ-like life must be entirely and absolutely himself, and taken as my types not merely the shepherd on the hillside and the prisoner in his cell but also the painter to whom the world is a pageant and the poet for whom the world is a song.[51]

4
Stories

Wilde's stories, discussed below, appeared between 1887 and 1891, the poems in prose in 1893 and 1894. *The Picture of Dorian Gray* was first published in June 1890. Within this span of eight years came also the four comedies, *Salomé*, and the fragmentary *A Florentine Tragedy* and *La Sainte Courtisane*. This flow of creativity makes systematic comment difficult. Most divisions may seem arbitrary; those of form are relatively clear-cut, at least superficially, so long as one is alert to the essential unity of Wilde's writings.

One common element which all the fictional narratives share is Wilde's development of his prose medium. In 1890, Wilde recalled Pater's question, 'Why do you always write poetry? Why do you not write prose? Prose is so much more difficult.'[1] The fashioning of his prose was clearly a major preoccupation for Wilde. Yeats, introducing a collection of Wilde's stories, placed a higher value on the oral: 'The further Wilde goes in his writings from the method of speech, from improvisation, from sympathy with some especial audience, the less original he is, the less accomplished.'[2] This judgment sets a higher value on *The Happy Prince and other Tales* than on the 'over-decorated', because written, stories of *A House of Pomegranates*. Vyvyan Holland recorded that his father 'would keep us quiet by telling us fairy stories, or tales of adventure, of which he had a never-ending supply . . . He told us all his own written fairy stories suitably adapted for our young minds, and a great many others as well.'[3] While the stories in *The Happy Prince* are generally more adaptable for children, and simpler in conception, there is little justification for considering them as in some way purer, less artificial, than what followed. In a letter to W. E. Henley, Wilde admits his major influence: 'Quite right, my dear "Marsyas et Apollo"; to learn how to write English prose I have studied the prose of France . . . Yes! Flaubert is my master, and when I get on with my translation of the *Tentation* I shall be Flaubert II, *Roi par grâce de Dieu*, and I hope something else beyond.'[4] Throughout, these stories represent highly conscious experiments in language.

It is part of Wilde's distinctiveness that his work is difficult to categorise. The Oxford *Complete Shorter Fiction of Oscar Wilde* begins with 'Lord Arthur Savile's Crime' and ends with one of the poems in prose, 'The Teacher of Wisdom', a wide enough range of tone even when only the titles are considered. Wilde at first referred to *The Picture of Dorian Gray* as his 'first long story';[5] in its expanded version, it became a novel. *The Happy Prince and other Tales* received varying definitions in the letters Wilde sent to accompany complimentary copies: 'It is only a collection of short stories, and is really meant for children . . .';[6] 'They are studies in prose, put for Romance's sake into a fanciful form: meant partly for children, and partly for those who have kept the childlike faculties of wonder and joy . . .';[7] 'my little book of fairy stories . . .'[8] When *A House of Pomegranates* was published three years later, in November 1891, a collection which included 'The Young King' and 'The Birthday of the Infanta' and which bore, at least superficially, some resemblance to the previous volume, Wilde savaged the reviewer of the *Pall Mall Gazette* for 'asking an extremely silly question, and that is, whether or not I have written this book for the purpose of giving pleasure to the British child'.[9]

The formal description of his works mattered to Wilde, in much the same way that the cover designs and illustrations and type contributed to the total effect. Wilde was never more serious than when engaged on the apparently slight or trivial. What gives unity to the fictional work referred to in this chapter is the story form. Wilde thought in stories, just as the Artist in the poem in prose of that title 'could only think in bronze'. Gide records Wilde telling him a version of 'The Artist' as a way of responding to a critic's misconception that Wilde invented tales to clothe his thought. Gide's comment that 'Wilde did not converse: he narrated' aligns with witnesses like W. Graham Robertson, who valued the stories Wilde told orally more highly than in their written form. Yeats, among many others, has described the peculiar qualities of Wilde's conversation: 'I never before heard a man talking with perfect sentences, as if he had written them all overnight with labour and yet all spontaneous.' Yeats, like Gide, contrives to praise and faintly disparage at the same time: 'Only when he spoke, or when his writing was the mirror of his speech, or in some simple fairy tale, had he words exact enough to hold a subtle ear.'[10] It may be that Wilde's fictional writing mirrored his speech more clearly than the other forms he used. The stories, whether satirical or mystical, are marvellously shaped for transmission by the spoken voice, and it is easy to understand how they evolved through numerous performed versions and variations before being constricted to print. Their intrinsic value, however, is far greater than merely that of traces or deposits of Wilde's conversational brilliance and charm. With their qualities of economy, clarity, and a capacity both to surprise and delight, they constitute a substantial achievement.

Lord Arthur Savile's Crime and Other Stories was published in July, 1891, and contained, apart from the title story, 'The Canterville Ghost' and two shorter pieces, 'The Sphinx without a Secret' and 'The Model Millionaire'. All appeared first in magazines during 1887. 'A Study of Cheiromancy', the sub-title of 'Lord Arthur Savile's Crime' on its initial publication in the *Court and Society Review*, became 'A Study of Duty' in 1891. This change serves to clarify the story's tone. It begins as an occasional piece, the description of Lady Windermere's reception at Bentinck House providing the original readers with a slightly sardonic image of a world either familiar to them, or with which they are flatteringly assumed to be familiar:

Gorgeous peeresses chatted affably to violent Radicals, popular preachers brushed coat-tails with eminent sceptics, a perfect bevy of bishops kept following a stout prima-donna from room to room, on the staircase stood several Royal Academicians, disguised as artists, and it was said that at one time the supper-room was absolutely crammed with geniuses.[11]

The incidental irony is relatively unobtrusive – the Royal Academicians 'disguised as artists', for instance; but the cumulative ironic intention becomes more apparent as the list proceeds from the opening two paradoxical juxtapositions (Gorgeous peeresses/violent Radicals, popular preachers/eminent sceptics) through the sham churchmen and artists to that condemnatory 'it was said'. The apparently familiar reality that Wilde is evoking is in his hands a fictional make-believe society, whose moving spirit, Lady Windermere, is herself described as a type of fairy-tale princess:

She looked wonderfully beautiful with her grand ivory throat, her large blue forget-me-not eyes, and her heavy coils of golden hair.

Lady Windermere, like the bevy of bishops, may not be quite what she seems:

She had more than once changed her husband; indeed, Debrett credits her with three marriages; but as she had never changed her lover, the world had long ago ceased to talk scandal about her.[12]

Lady Windermere's latest 'lion' is a cheiromantist, whose comic name of Podgers suggests his role as house buffoon. He reads a few hands, progressing in his interpretations from the banal to the faintly disturbing. But when he sees Lord Arthur Savile's hand, a violent change occurs: 'huge beads of perspiration broke out on his yellow forehead like a poisonous dew, and his fat fingers grew cold and clammy'.[13] It is a moment that comes from melodrama, and seems to invite an accompaniment of menacing chords from the orchestra pit. Lord Arthur, as he privately learns later, is destined to commit a murder.

The focus changes to Lord Arthur, the perfect flower of the English aristocracy. After a night spent wandering through a hellish London townscape, he enjoys a luxurious bath, emerging from it as though newly baptised to assume his responsibility. The paragraphs which follow provide the dynamics of the story. Lord Arthur, engaged to Miss Sibyl Merton, conceives it as his moral duty to commit the murder before the wedding. 'He felt that to marry her, with the doom of murder hanging over his head, would be a betrayal like that of Judas, a sin worse than any the Borgia had ever dreamed of.'[14] He decides on a victim, an elderly cousin, Lady Clementina Beauchamp, but she dies a natural death without recourse to the *bonbon* of aconitine he has procured for her; his uncle the Dean of Chichester escapes the attentions of an exploding clock; finally, he chances on Podgers leaning over the parapet of the Thames by Cleopatra's Needle, and tips him into the river.

Wilde provides this mechanically perfect, coolly ironic tale with a crystalline after-piece. The marriage between Lord Arthur and Sybil Merton duly takes place, and the bride and bridegroom are supremely happy. 'Never for a single moment did Lord Arthur regret all that he had suffered for Sybil's sake . . .'[15] Moreover, this happiness is presented as continuing. Some years later, Lady Windermere visits the couple in their 'lovely old place' in the country. Sitting under the lime-tree, watching the two beautiful children playing in the rose-walk, she asks Sybil if she is happy. Sybil's state of rural happiness is contrasted with the London season's artificial distractions, such as the late and unlamented Podgers. Lord Arthur, arriving with 'a large bunch of yellow roses', and his children dancing around him, is asked if he believes in cheiromancy. He replies first that he owes to it 'all the happiness of my life', and then, pressed further by Lady Windermere:

'My dear Lord Arthur, what do you owe to it?'
'Sybil', he answered, handing his wife the roses, and looking into her
violet eyes.

This bland and conventionally sentimental close is qualified both
by the accumulated moral ambiguity of the preceding story, and
immediately by the disclaimer of Lady Windermere, who spon-
taneously provides the conventional, modern judgment on the
secret crime that has secured Lord Arthur's happiness:

'What nonsense!' cried Lady Windermere. 'I never heard such nonsense
in all my life.'[16]

In terms of Wilde's future writing, 'Lord Arthur Savile's
Crime' contains a number of interesting signposts. Wilde reflects
his own work more than most authors, both in superficial detail
such as names (Lady Windermere), epigrams and short descrip-
tive passages, and in more substantial ways. For example, the
evening reception with which the story opens may be seen as a
preliminary sketch for the more elaborate scenes in *Lady
Windermere's Fan* (Act Two) or *An Ideal Husband* (Act One).

More central is the London nightscape, which carries considerable metaphoric and psychological importance:

Then he wandered across Oxford Street into narrow, shameful alleys.
Two women with painted faces mocked at him as he went by. From a
dark courtyard came a sound of oaths and blows, followed by shrill
screams, and, huddled upon a damp doorstep, he saw the crook-backed
forms of poverty and eld. A strange pity came over him. Were these
children of sin and misery predestined to their end, as he to his? Were
they, like him, merely the puppets of a monstrous show?[17]

This vision of the city's pain recalls the images of Wilde's poem
'The Harlot's House', published in April 1885, and shares, too,
the poem's spareness and precision:

> Sometimes a horrible marionette
> Came out, and smoked its cigarette
> Upon the steps like a live thing.[18]

Later in his odyssey, Lord Arthur confronts his own crime, a bill
on a hoarding with 'the word "Murder", printed in black letters'.
At the end of his night's wandering, he encounters at dawn
the return of daytime innocence in the form of a modern
Arcadia:

As he strolled home towards Belgrave Square, he met the great waggons
on their way to Covent Garden. The white-smocked carters, with their
pleasant sunburnt faces and coarse curly hair, strode sturdily on, cracking
their whips, and calling out now and then to each other; on the back of
a huge grey horse, the leader of a jangling team, sat a chubby boy, with
a bunch of primroses in his battered hat, keeping tight hold of the mane
with his little hands, and laughing; and the great piles of vegetables looked
like masses of jade against the morning sky, like masses of green jade
against the pink petals of some marvellous rose.[19]

The night/day, sin/innocence conjunction was explored in similar
vein in Wilde's Whistlerian poem 'Impression du Matin':

> Then suddenly arose the clang
> Of waking life; the streets were stirred
> With country waggons: and a bird
> Flew to the glistening roofs and sang.
>
> But one pale woman all alone,
> The daylight kissing her wan hair,
> Loitered beneath the gas lamps' flare,
> With lips of flame and heart of stone.[20]

The association of the dark London underworld with death, of
body and soul, was developed by Wilde in *The Picture of Dorian
Gray*, Chapter 7, though without any sense of relief or consolation
at the break of dawn. In 'Lord Arthur Savile's Crime' Wilde provides Lord Arthur with a fairy-tale solution. The absurd coin-
cidence of Podgers's presence, and the farcical interjection of the
policeman as the cheiromantist's body is borne away down the
Thames, 'Have you dropped anything, sir?', anticipate the comic
technique of Stoppard and Orton.[21] Within Wilde's own work,
the story is a prelude to *The Importance of Being Earnest*. The connection is formed not so much by particular motifs as by Wilde's
consistent command of comic tone, and by his ability to create a
fictional world that is demonstrably related to the social setting
inhabited by his readers and yet one which apparently functions,
in terms of success and happiness, on a reversed, indeed perverse,
moral system. As in the later comedy, Wilde simply offers,
without comment, his ironic vision of the world with its concluding image of an English Eden entered after a health-giving
bite from the fruit of the tree of knowledge.

'The Canterville Ghost' first appeared a few months earlier
than 'Lord Arthur Savile's Crime'. Equally designed to entertain,
it has less resonance. Its targets are either more purely literary, or

concerned with manners rather than behaviour. Hiram B. Otis, the American minister, buys Canterville Chase from Lord Canterville, and acquires the ghost along with the furniture. The first four sections concern the ghost's efforts to assert himself in the face of the relentless scepticism of the Otis family. He is insulted with patent remedies for his creaking chains and demoniac laughter, and bombarded with pillows and booby-traps by the Otis sons. In the fifth section, however, the story's hitherto hectic mood and pace slows and becomes solemn. Virginia, the gentle fifteen-year-old Otis daughter, encounters the ghost sitting by the window, 'watching the ruined gold of the yellowing trees fly through the air, and the red leaves dancing madly down the long avenue'.[22] Though the echoes of Tennyson and Coleridge signal a parody of romanticism, and the ensuing conversation maintains the light note of earlier sequences, the mood gradually modulates into a solemn mysticism more common in the later fairy-stories. Virginia, who begins by castigating the ghost for his wickedness, learns that he has not slept for 300 years:

'Poor, poor Ghost,' she murmured; 'have you no place where you can sleep?'
'Far away beyond the pinewoods,' he answered, in a low dreamy voice, 'there is a little garden . . .'[23]

Virginia recognises the place from the description as the Garden of Death, and agrees to accompany the ghost into the darkness, and so fulfil the old prophecy painted on the library window:

> When a golden girl can win
> Prayer from out the lips of sin,
> When the barren almond bears,
> And the little child gives away its tears,
> Then shall all the house be still
> And peace come to Canterville.

Virginia successfully lays the ghost to rest – he is given Christian burial in the churchyard – and returns to the material world with a box of jewels. Her other reward, like that of 'All good little American girls', is a Duchess's coronet. The story, like 'Lord Arthur Savile's Crime', ends serenely, with one of those Wildean affirmations that sits less comfortably in this context than in the next two collections:

He made me see what Life is, and what Death signifies, and why Love is stronger than both.[24]

In spite of those grave-seeming capitals, Wilde has by this juncture largely succeeded in reasserting the initial light comedic tone by the arguments between Mr Otis and Lord Canterville over the possession of the jewels, and by the immediately preceding description of the marriage. The story, as a whole, relies on two main sources of humour. The first, a legacy of his lecture tour, is the gentle satire of the American way of life (pragmatic, materialistic, land of 'Pinkerton's Champion Stain Remover and Paragon Detergent', clam-bakes, and belief in the cultural importance of Boston), balanced by the puncturing of English pretension by the honesty of the American Puritan tradition (a method repeated by Wilde through the character of Hester Worsley in *A Woman of No Importance*). The second source is Wilde's light-fingered skill in referring to a wide range of literary forms. Most obvious is the Gothic novel, for instance in the description of Canterville Chase and its housekeeper, Mrs Umney:

She made them each a low curtsey as they alighted, and said in a quaint, old-fashioned manner, 'I bid you welcome to Canterville Chase.'[25]

Wilde extends his Gothic references to the more outrageous manifestations of Victorian melodrama, in a running gag of the ghost's most famous roles as they might be described on play-bills, such as 'Gaunt Gibeon, the Blood-sucker of Bexley Moor' or 'Black Isaac, or the Huntsman of Hogley Woods'. The story may glance at Henry James's *The Portrait of a Lady*, whose American heroine Isabel Archer is also given an encounter with a ghost. In addition, Poe, Longfellow, Shakespeare and *The Song of Solomon* feature among Wilde's referents. The sophisticated use Wilde makes of literary genres, mocking them and yet relying upon them, contributes to the feeling that in this instance he has successfully created a sub-genre of his own. Like 'The Birthday of the Infanta', 'The Canterville Ghost' has been adapted successfully as a ballet, a form which absorbs with ease both the solemnity and pathos of the innocent girl's initiation by the ghost, and its juxtaposition with the conventions of a comedy of modern manners.

The Happy Prince and other Tales (comprising, after the title story, 'The Nightingale and the Rose', 'The Selfish Giant', 'The Devoted Friend' and 'The Remarkable Rocket') was published in 1888, with illustrations by Walter Crane and Jacomb Hood. It is a remarkably homogeneous collection, and the tales, like the best children's stories, have a wide appeal. Here, as always, Wilde has drawn on many authors, sources and traditions. Hans Christian

Andersen is the most obvious and pervasive, both in technique and theme, while Tennyson's 'The Palace of Art' is 'the definitive statement of the dilemma around which Wilde's tales revolve'.[26] This general dilemma might be stated broadly as a recognition, first, of the price paid in human suffering for beauty, art, power and wealth, and of the corresponding salvation offered by sacrificial love. The theme of selfless sacrifice is prominent in the first four stories; Wilde's major target is egotism, culminating in the supreme vanity of the Rocket.

'The Happy Prince' contains two examples of sacrifice: the statue of the Happy Prince, who gives away the ruby on his sword-hilt, his sapphire eyes and his gold-leaf in order to alleviate the distress and poverty he sees in the city below, and whose leaden heart finally snaps in two; and the Swallow, who stays behind in the north to carry out the Prince's wishes and dies of cold. These acts of selfless love are elevated at the story's close:

'Bring me the two most precious things in the city,' said God to one of His Angels; and the Angels brought Him the leaden heart and the dead bird.[27]

The sudden introduction of God shifts the story towards parable, especially since the materialist city world has utterly failed to perceive the significance of the Happy Prince's transformation, throwing the lead heart on to a dust-heap to join the dead Swallow. The brisk insensitivity of the human characters – or at least the powerful and learned among them – gives 'The Happy Prince' a tone of scepticism. Wilde keeps his sentimental tendencies largely under control. The generalised human targets – the Mayor, the Town Councillors, the Mathematical Master, the Watchman – are picked off with dry economy and precision, while the recipients of the Happy Prince's gifts remain unaware of his generosity and behave in a realistically ungrateful manner. The artist-Student's reaction to finding the sapphire in his garret is characteristic:

'I am beginning to be appreciated,' he cried; 'this is from some great admirer. Now I can finish my play,' and he looked quite happy.[28]

The hint of reservation achieved through that 'quite' is typical of Wilde's low-key method. In the sphere of moral direction he works by implication rather than by statement. He also uses a number of contrasts to striking effect: the Prince and the Swallow, the Swallow and his lover the Reed, the present and the past (as evoked by the statue of the Prince and his recollections of 'when I was alive'), the rich and the poor, the northern city and the Egypt of the warm south. This last is an important structural element, for Wilde employs it to point up the three moral decisions which the Swallow has to make, weighing the immediacy of the poor's predicament against the romantic, alluring images of Egypt, the Egypt of Flaubert and of Gautier's poem 'Ce Que Disent Les Hirondelles'. As the Prince tells the Swallow, 'you tell me of marvellous things, but more marvellous than anything is the suffering of men and of women'.[29] Recognition of such suffering was a recurring impulse and theme with Wilde. In 'The Happy Prince' he finds an ideal form to present the mystery, without attempting to offer a solution.

The ostensible theme of 'The Nightingale and the Rose' is sacrifice, or selfless love. The Student yearns for a red rose, so that his love will dance with him at the Prince's ball. The Nightingale, thinking she has at last identified the true lover she has sung of so often, seeks for a red rose to give him; learning that she must 'build it out of music by moonlight, and stain it with your own heart's blood',[30] she sacrifices her life in order to create it. When the girl rejects the proffered rose, the Student discards it and returns to his dusty books. As the story unfolds, however, it is clear that the focus lies less in any moral implication than in providing an image of the process of art: the supreme act of artistic creation, it is suggested, involves the suffering, indeed the extinction, of the artist:

So the Nightingale pressed closer against the thorn, and the thorn touched her heart, and a fierce pang of pain shot through her. Bitter, bitter was the pain, and wilder and wilder grew her song, for she sang of the Love that is perfected by Death, of the Love that dies not in the tomb.[31]

Ironically, only the moonlit world of nature hears and responds to the song: the moon, the rose tree, the reeds of the river. The rose itself, though recognised as unique by the Student, immediately becomes subject to scientific classification: 'It is so beautiful that I am sure it has a long Latin name'; while the girl rejects it in favour of jewels, and because it will not go with her dress. The rejection of the rose is also the rejection of love. Wilde, for once, offers, if only momentarily, the clearest interpretation:

The nightingale is the true lover, if there is one. She, at least, is Romance, and the student and the girl are, like most of us, unworthy of Romance. So, at least, it seems to me, but I like to fancy that there may be many meanings in the tale, for in writing it I did not start with an idea and clothe it in form, but began with a form and strove to make it beautiful enough to have many secrets and many answers.[32]

The secrets and answers may not be so numerous as Wilde implies, but the emphasis on form is surely apt. It is the pattern and balance and rhythm of the story which fix it in the imagination.

'Beauty and tenderness' were the qualities in 'The Selfish Giant' remarked upon by Walter Pater, who called it 'perfect in its kind'[33] (a useful phrase for a generous reviewer). It is a little difficult to know what 'kind' Pater had in mind. The first part of the story is effective, with the extreme simplicity of the fable enlivened by flashes of wit and tart, vigorous phrasing. The Giant suffers satisfactorily for his selfishness in excluding the children from his garden. The central, transitional section, with the children creeping back into the garden through a hole in the wall, and the Giant's heart melted by a boy too small to climb up into a tree, is written in an unmistakably biblical syntax and rhythm:

And the tree broke at once into blossom, and the birds came and sang on it, and the little boy stretched out his two arms and flung them round the Giant's neck, and kissed him.[34]

In the third section, when the Giant approaches death, the boy is transformed abruptly and blatantly into the figure of Christ. The restraining thread of wit is, naturally enough, discarded; the language becomes mechanical, and the tone verges on the mawkish.

'The Devoted Friend' and 'The Remarkable Rocket' are relatively confined in range. The first, reminiscent of Andersen in its use of an animal framework for the central story, is a cautionary tale about friendship. Little Hans is horribly exploited by his friend the rich Miller, who is a pleasantly sardonic study both of a supreme egotist and of the gulf between words and action: 'Lots of people act well,' as the Miller puts it, 'but very few people talk well, which shows that talking is much the more difficult thing of the two . . .'[35] Wilde increases the comic effect by matching the Miller with an equally self-satisfied Water-rat in the outer frame who fails to see the 'moral' in the story. 'The Remarkable Rocket' is another study in vanity. The classic formula of animating a collection of objects, in this case fireworks, within the context of the wedding celebrations of a fairy-tale prince and princess is exploited brilliantly by Wilde as he lightly satirises a range of social attitudes, alluding perhaps to the

Ruskin–Whistler controversy. At the same time he moves the narration swiftly towards an appropriate anti-climax.

The stories in this collection, with the possible exception of 'The Selfish Giant', are written with a distinctive blend of simplicity and sophistication. The writing is economical, with clear syntax, short paragraphs and a restricted range of vocabulary. Certain features, though, are more obviously directed at an adult readership, for instance the ideas about art in 'The Nightingale and the Rose', and the comedy of manners in 'The Remarkable Rocket'. Wilde's general artistic intentions in these stories are explained by him in the following terms: 'an attempt to mirror modern life in a form remote from reality – to deal with modern problems in a mode that is ideal and not imitative';[36] and (of 'The Happy Prince') 'an attempt to treat a tragic modern problem in a form that aims at delicacy and imaginative treatment: it is a reaction against the purely imitative character of modern art'.[37] These comments connect the practice of the tales with the critical attitude developed in 'The Decay of Lying', especially in Wilde's strictures on modern novelists, who fall so readily into 'careless habits of accuracy': 'if something cannot be done to check, or at least to modify, our monstrous worship of facts, Art will become sterile, and Beauty will pass away from the land'.[38] The tales, as defined above by Wilde, certainly conform to Vivian's second doctrine: 'All bad art comes from returning to Life and Nature, and elevating them into ideals.'[34] Whether they meet the first doctrine of the 'new' aesthetics, 'Art never expresses anything but itself', is less clear. The tales seem closer in spirit to Wilde's definition of the objectivity of art in 'The English Renaissance': 'Art never harms itself by keeping aloof from the social problems of the day: rather, by so doing, it more completely realises for us that which we desire.'[40] In fact, 'The Devoted Friend' itself warns against too close a connection between art and life:

'I am rather afraid that I have annoyed him', answered the Linnet. 'The fact is, that I told him a story with a moral.'

'Ah! that is always a very dangerous thing to do,' said the Duck.

And I quite agree with her.[41]

The unobserved climactic explosion of 'The Remarkable Rocket', placed pointedly at the end of the collection, similarly inhibits all but the most lightly allusive kind of interpretation.

With *A House of Pomegranates*, Wilde is more consciously using the form of fairy-tale to address himself to an adult audience. 'The Young King' is in part a development from 'The Happy Prince'. The Young King (the child of an artist) at first enjoys the beauty of the palace of Joyeuse, just as the Happy Prince did during his lifetime within the sanctuary of his Palace of Sans-Souci. But Wilde now substantially expands and decorates his vision of the world of art and beauty:

The walls were hung with rich tapestries representing the Triumph of Beauty. A large press, inlaid with agate and lapis-lazuli, filled one corner, and facing the window stood a curiously wrought cabinet with lacquer panels of powdered and mosaiced gold, on which were placed some delicate goblets of Venetian glass, and a cup of dark-veined onyx.[42]

This chamber of Beauty is the setting for the Young King's three dreams on the eve of his coronation, dreams in which he is shown the price in human suffering that is paid to achieve his coronation robes and jewels. The implications of the dreams are dismissed by the courtiers, the people, and even by the Bishop; but when the Young King, mocked by his subjects for the poverty of his shepherd's cloak, stands before the image of Christ which hangs above the altar, he is miraculously transformed by the Glory of God. The implications of the Christian–Socialist message are clear. Their impact is the greater because of the realistic questioning of them which Wilde puts into the mouths of the King's subjects, arguments that had been well-rehearsed in Victorian industrialised society: 'To toil for a hard master is bitter, but to have no master to toil for is more bitter still.'[43] Again, 'The Palace of Art' forms part of the story's frame of reference, but the reverse images, the 'white-eyed phantasms weeping tears of blood', are powerfully realised by Wilde through the medium of the dreams, to which the vision of the final paragraph forms a justified counterpoint.

'The Birthday of the Infanta' stands out from the other stories, in that it has no obvious analogues. Wilde has created a self-standing, imaginary world whose inspiration is visual rather than literary, anchored on Velasquez's paintings of the Spanish court. It is less dependent on narrative than the other stories, and is built around the antithesis of Art and Nature, of outward and spiritual beauty, expressed through the contrast between the beautiful but cruel Infanta, the product of civilisation, and the ugly, warm-natured Dwarf, who dies of a broken heart. The tale is organised into an introduction followed by three main phases, or scenes.

First, there is the account of the Infanta's birthday entertainments, with the Dwarf's dancing as the climax. The previous
acts have been miracles of artifice. The puppets, who perform
Sophonisba, 'acted so well, and their gestures were so extremely
natural, that at the close of play the eyes of the Infanta were quite
dim with tears';[44] and it seemed intolerable to the Grand In-
quisitor that things made simply out of wood and coloured wax,
and worked mechanically by wires, should be so unhappy and
meet with such terrible misfortunes. The Dwarf, however, is
totally natural and unselfconscious, having no awareness of his
grotesque appearance. When the children laugh at him, he laughs
with them, and accepts the white rose the Infanta throws at him
as a serious tribute. In the second phase, the Dwarf is in the palace
garden. Wilde develops the idea of his natural goodness. Initially,
he draws a contrast between the disdainful attitude of the
cultivated Flowers towards the Dwarf and the sympathy of the
Birds and the Lizards. Then, the Dwarf imagines that he is introducing the Infanta to the pleasures of the forest. Within this
idyll one harsh note intrudes: the Dwarf innocently recollects a
'beautiful procession', whose centre is three bare-footed men en
route in reality to the inquisition at Toledo.

In the third phase, the Dwarf enters the Palace to search for the
Infanta and ask her to accompany him to the forest. Here the
emphasis is placed by Wilde on the building's decorative
magnificence. But in this Palace of Art the Dwarf finally sees, in
a mirror, his own self-image, and dies of grief at his ugliness as
the Infanta and her companions watch and laugh at his 'acting'.
The story's ending is as chilling as the conclusion of *The Picture of
Dorian Gray*, and recalls the incomprehension of the citizens in
'The Happy Prince':

'But why will he not dance again?' asked the Infanta, laughing.

'Because his heart is broken,' answered the Chamberlain.

And the Infanta frowned, and her dainty rose-leaf lips curled in pretty dis-
dain. 'For the future let those who come to play with me have no hearts,'
she cried, and she ran out into the garden.[45]

The Infanta's command picks up the melancholy tone which per-
meates the introduction, particularly in the description of her own
father's doomed love for his young Queen, which gives a sense of
context and dimension to the Infanta's cold cruelty. The opposition of Infanta and Dwarf, the visual brilliance of the court setting,

and the poignancy of the scene before the mirror, have been vividly realised in ballet. The story, perfect in form and execution, articulates a disturbing critique of Art, all the more startling because of its apparent contradiction to Wilde's public stance.

'The Fisherman and his Soul' is in some ways the most substantial, complex and significant of these stories. It begins in a manner familiar from Andersen or Arnold, with the Fisherman in love with a Mermaid, a love which can only be fulfilled if the Fisherman sends away his Soul. It is in describing the Fisherman's efforts to dispose of his Soul that Wilde expands the story's circle of meaning. The Priest whom he consults drives him from his door; the merchants mock him. A young witch, reminiscent of a Yeatsian dancer, invites him to a Sabbath, where she swears to tell him the secret of disposing of one's Soul in exchange for a dance; during the Sabbath the Fisherman reveals his innate goodness by making the sign of the cross in the presence of the devil. At this stage the story has some affinity with *The Picture of Dorian Gray*, as the Fisherman consciously cuts away his Soul, while retaining his heart. The next section, traditionally tripartite in form, concerns the Soul's efforts to return to the Fisherman. The Soul tempts him with wisdom, riches, and finally with the image of another dancer, which lures the Fisherman from the sea, so that his Soul may be united with him. Wilde further increases the complexity of the fable by making a distinction between the heart and the Soul. The Fisherman's heart remains with the Mermaid, though he is separated from her. The Soul, sent into the world without a heart, has learned to love evil. It is not until the sea bears the Mermaid's dead body to the Fisherman's feet, and he kisses her lips, that his heart breaks and allows the Soul to be 'one with him even as before'. Finally, the Body/Soul opposition is restated in the epilogue, when the Priest is led to bless the sea. Wilde adds a typically deflationary last sentence: 'Nor came the Sea-folk into the bay as they had been wont to do, for they went to another part of the sea.'[46] As with 'The Birthday of the Infanta', the vision of goodness is revealed, and then withdrawn.

A similarly sombre note is struck at the end of 'The Star Child', who, so great has been his suffering, rules for only three years before his death: 'And he who came after him ruled evilly.'[47] This story, markedly biblical in the cadences of the sentences, as in word and phrase, is like a Romantic re-interpretation of the

Sermon on the Mount, but one which lacks the promise of eternal life. It is concerned with the relationship between physical and spiritual beauty, and the crucial actions are those of pity and cruelty: the good woodcutter and his wife who take up the Star Child, in contrast to his hard-hearted companion; the Star Child's cruelty to wild creatures, and his denial of his mother in the form of a beggar-woman; and his acts of reparation, first in rescuing the hare from the trap, and secondly in giving three pieces of gold to the leper. The Star Child has three physical states: an initial beauty, his body significantly 'like the narcissus of a field where the mower comes not',[48] which is the accompaniment to his youthful cruelty; a physical ugliness, 'as foul as the toad, and as loathsome as the adder', which comes upon him when he rejects his mother; and a final transformation after his third act of pity, when he looks at his reflection from a shield: 'his comeliness had come back to him, and he saw that in his eyes which he had not seen there before'.[49]

Apart from the ubiquitous influence of the Authorised Version of the Bible, Wilde also owes something to Flaubert's *La Légende de Saint Julien l'Hospitalier*, in which Julien, as a child, commits a series of gratuitously cruel actions against animals and birds, until he becomes obsessed by slaughter.

'The Portrait of Mr W. H.' is an unusual and individual work, part story, part critical essay, part confessional. It shares a common theme with the prose-poem 'The Teacher of Wisdom', the idea that convincing another of what one believes leads to loss of faith on one's own part. Its use of the portrait motif, almost indeed a 'poison' portrait, aligns it with *The Picture of Dorian Gray*. Its literary and aesthetic concerns recall those of Wilde's critical essays; at one point he suggested that Blackwood might publish it in a volume together with 'The Decay of Lying' and 'Pen, Pencil and Poison'. The central thesis, that the 'W. H.' of the dedication to Shakespeare's sonnets was an Elizabethan boy actor, Willie Hughes, was both an ingenious comment on pedantic Shakespearean scholarship, providing an explanation more credible than many, and a covert declaration of his own homosexual inclinations. Blackwood, who accepted the story for his magazine, commented to Wilde that 'the Shakespearean theory possesses much playful ingenuity'.[50] Elkin Mathew's refusal, in 1894, to publish it 'at any price'[51] represents a more worldly and suspicious reaction. It is a *jeu d'esprit*, more successful in its shorter original form than in the expanded version not published until

1921. The forged, fatal portrait which is linked with the suicide of
the original theorist, Cyril Graham, – 'the only perfect Rosalind
I have ever seen'[52] – and the faked suicide of his friend and successor Erskine, survives as an ominous witness on the walls of the
narrator's library. The narrator professes a sceptical objectivity:
'To die for one's theological beliefs is the worst use a man can
make of his life, but to die for a literary theory! It seemed impossible.'[53] Wilde's skill is to make the apparently impossible seem
uncomfortably plausible.

The story form, through which Wilde expressed so many and
varied impulses and purposes, achieved one further development
in his work, the poem in prose. If Flaubert was Wilde's master in
the stories, here Baudelaire provided the inspiration. Only six
were published out of the great number which, by many accounts,
he used to tell when he conversed or, as Gide described, narrated.
They are related to *De Profundis*, in that they seem to reveal the
speaking voice with the minimum interposition of literary form
between Wilde and the reader. 'The Disciple', a reversal of the
Narcissus legend, has something of the paradoxical nature of an
epigram. 'The Artist', who 'could only think in bronze', possesses
a similarly epigrammatic conclusion:

And out of the image of *The Sorrow that endureth for Ever* he fashioned an
image of *The Pleasure that abideth for a Moment.*[54]

Confronted with that kind of statement, one is tempted to read the
poems in prose as confessional. 'The Doer of Good', 'The
Master' and 'The House of Judgement' are concerned with Christian belief, or rather with the difficulties of belief; while 'The
Teacher of Wisdom', the longest, explores the distinction between
the knowledge and the love of God. The interest displayed by
Wilde in the person and teaching of Christ prompted him both to
identify himself with Christ (as in *De Profundis*) and to teach in
something which approaches the form of a parable.

These poems in prose represent a most unusual achievement.
The biblical echoes of the language and cadences seem highly
appropriate to the form and subject-matter. The approximation to
parable leads one to expect the possibility of interpretation, of the
emergence of moral or aesthetic principle. Instead, the poems tend
to conclude in perfectly balanced paradox, or, since paradox has
connotations of the wrong kind of wit, simply in perfect yet
disconcerting balance. In 'The House of Judgement', the Man comes

before God, who three times opens the Book of the Life of the Man
and reads to him the evil he has done.

And the Man made answer and said, 'Even so did I.'
And God closed the Book of the Life of the Man, and said, 'Surely I will
send thee into Hell. Even into Hell will I send thee.'
And the Man cried out, 'Thou canst not.'
And God said to the Man, 'Wherefore can I not send thee to hell, and
for what reason?'
'Because in Hell have I always lived,' answered the Man.
And there was silence in the House of Judgement.
And after a space God spake, and said to the Man, 'Seeing that I may
not send thee into Hell, surely I will send thee unto Heaven. Even unto
Heaven will I send thee.'
And the Man cried out, 'Thou canst not.'
And God said to the Man, 'Wherefore can I not send thee unto Heaven,
and for what reason?'
'Because never, and in no place, have I been able to imagine it,' answered
the Man.
And there was silence in the House of Judgement.[55]

If nothing else, this poem in prose demonstrates Wilde's range,
when placed beside 'Lord Arthur Savile's Crime'. It is, too, an
example of the way Wilde would explore and refine a particular
tone or form until he had perfected or exhausted it: the tone is that
of a Teacher of Wisdom, the artist/critic as prophetic symbol, but
what he expresses is bleakly modern, even absurdist – Beckett's
deployment of stories and parables in *Waiting for Godot* and
Endgame comes to mind. The ironic pessimism of this particular
vision counterpointed by the burnished language in which it is
expressed is a technique taken further by Wilde in, most notably,
the dramatic mode of *Salomé*.

Peter Raby
Oscar Wilde
N.Y
1988
Cambrige Univ. Press

5

The Picture of Dorian Gray

Wilde's novel *The Picture of Dorian Gray* originated as a story for *Lippincott's Magazine*, where it was published in the July number, 1890. In this form, it consisted of fourteen chapters, which represented a sustained effort of concentration for Wilde: 'I have just finished my first long story, and am tired out. I am afraid it is rather like my own life – all conversation and no action. I can't describe action: my people sit in chairs and chatter.'[1] The disclaimer is not strictly accurate. Even in the original version the story contains three deaths, including a suicide and a murder. Nevertheless, the limited space given to action, together with Wilde's abrupt, idiosyncratic handling of it, makes a noticeable feature of both versions, and raises questions as to the nature of the work, and how it was intended to be understood.

It was, inevitably, misunderstood, and Wilde turned his energies to constructing public replies to his critics, in particular those of the *St James's Gazette* and the *Scots Observer*. Wilde's first response included the declaration that he was 'quite incapable of understanding how any work of art can be criticised from a moral standpoint'.[2] Such a statement, wholly to be expected from a writer such as Wilde, is none the less (and no doubt intentionally) ingenuous, given the form and subject matter of the book. The central idea consists of a beautiful young man 'selling his soul in exchange for eternal youth'; the portrait, which is the physical representation of his soul, reflects Dorian Gray's sins; Dorian Gray himself confesses that he has been 'poisoned' by a book. It would be hard to avoid a certain amount of moral inference; Wilde admitted as much in a letter to the Editor of the *Daily Chronicle*: 'I felt that, from an aesthetic point of view, it would be difficult to keep the moral in its proper secondary place; and even now I do not feel quite sure that I have been able to do so. I think the moral too apparent.'[3] Wilde continued by defining the moral element:

The real moral of the story is that all excess, as well as all renunciation, brings its punishment, and this moral is so far artistically and deliberately suppressed that it does not enunciate its law as a general principle, but realises itself purely in the lives of individuals, and so becomes simply a dramatic element in a work of art, and not the object of the work of art itself.

An excessively prominent moral element was one of the things Wilde hoped to correct in revising and expanding the *Lippincott's* version. His aim had been to keep the 'atmosphere of moral corruption' surrounding Dorian Gray 'vague and indeterminate and wonderful': 'Each man sees his own sin in Dorian Gray.'[4] The indeterminate nature of Dorian's sins had already been assisted by J. M. Stoddart, the American publisher of *Lippincott's*, who had made numerous unauthorised deletions and substitutions. Wilde worked from the *Lippincott's* text, rather than from his original typescript, and only rarely reinstated his first version. One of his aims in the process of revision was to reduce the suggestions of homosexuality in the relationship between Basil Hallward and Dorian Gray, which he accomplished by stressing Dorian's importance for Hallward as artistic inspiration. At the same time, the inserted episodes such as Dorian's visit to the opium den in Chapter 16 have a greater specificity which runs counter to the claimed vagueness. In both versions the focus is not directed exclusively at either the aesthetic (Art) or the moral (Life), but at the tension between them.

The strength of *The Picture of Dorian Gray* derives primarily from the central and unifying idea of the picture itself. The artist Basil Hallward, obsessed and inspired by the youthful beauty of Dorian Gray, is about to complete his masterpiece, a full-length portrait. As Dorian poses, Lord Henry Wotton, the detached amoral observer, tempts him with words that stir him like music: 'Ah! realize your youth while you have it . . . Live the wonderful life that is in you! . . . Be always searching for new sensations.'[5] Soon, the portrait is finished – 'the finest portrait of modern times' – and when Dorian sees it, a look of joy comes into his eyes, 'as if he had recognised himself for the first time'. The sense of his own beauty comes on him like a revelation, and he expresses a fatal wish: 'If it were I who was to be always young, and the picture that was to grow old! . . . I would give my soul for that!'[6]

The picture has become endued with terrible significance: Lord Henry offers to buy it at any price; to its creator Hallward, it represents his aesthetic ideal, though he secretly fears that it contains too much of himself; to Dorian, it reveals the transitory nature of his beauty so acutely that he is jealous of it, as though it had a life of its own. When Hallward takes up a palette knife to destroy the work which threatens to mar their relationships, Dorian tears the knife from his hand, crying out that it would be murder. The picture is preserved, and promised to Dorian. But the relationship between Dorian and Hallward has altered crucially. It is now Lord Henry who is to become Dorian's mentor.

This opening episode, contained in Chapters 1 and 2, establishes two patterns which are structurally important. The first involves the knife: Dorian tears the palette knife from Hallward's grasp, preventing a symbolic murder; he stabs Hallward to death in front of the portrait in Chapter 13; ultimately, he stabs the picture with the same knife – 'As it had killed the painter, so it would kill the painter's work'[7] – and his own body is discovered with a knife in the heart. The second pattern is concerned with the relationship between Dorian's actions and the picture's appearance, which serves as a record of his soul's progress. The picture, initially, functions as a perfect image of his beauty, a beauty of soul as well as of feature. When Dorian rejects his love Sybil Vane – a rejection caused by her failure in the art of acting – and so precipitates her suicide, the picture's expression changes: 'One would have said that there was a touch of cruelty in the mouth';[8] after Hallward's murder, a 'loathsome red dew' 'gleamed, wet and glistening, on one of the hands, as though the canvas had sweated blood';[9] when Dorian commits a good action, by sparing the innocent Hetty Merton, he hopes the portrait may reflect his new life, but is horrified to find no change, 'save that in the eyes there was a look of cunning, and in the mouth the curved wrinkle of the hypocrite'.[10] Finally, at Dorian's death, the youth and beauty which have been miraculously preserved in him are transferred back to the portrait, while he himself becomes 'withered, wrinkled, and loathsome of visage'.[11]

Within the framework, and in addition to Dorian's relationships with Hallward and Lord Henry, who in places seem to function as good and evil angel to his Faustus, there are two major episodes. The first involves Dorian's passion for the actress Sibyl Vane. Sibyl, child-like and naive, acts 'all the great heroines of the world in one';[12] in a sordid little theatre, surrounded by third-rate players and grotesque scenery, she plays Juliet, Imogen, Rosalind, Ophelia, Desdemona. Dorian is entranced by her performance, and relates the nature of his happiness to Hallward and Lord Henry. (This act of confiding is frequently associated with danger in Wilde's writing, the process of convincing another leading to a failure of belief on the part of the speaker.) Sibyl was playing Rosalind, one of several glances at Gautier's Mademoiselle de Maupin, and a link also with Mr W. H. Significantly, Dorian defines Sibyl's qualities first in terms of art:

She had never seemed to me more exquisite. She had all the delicate grace of that Tanagra figurine that you have in your studio, Basil. Her hair clustered round her face like dark leaves round a pale rose. As for her acting – well, you shall see her tonight. She is simply a born artist.[13]

Next, he recounts the moment of ecstatic union:

As we were sitting together, suddenly there came into her eyes a look that I had never seen there before. My lips moved towards her. We kissed each other. I can't describe to you what I felt at that moment. It seemed to me that all my life had been narrowed to one perfect point of rose-coloured joy.[14]

It is noteworthy that Wilde presents this moment as reported rather than direct action, so that the emphasis is placed upon Dorian's attempt to define the experience. As though to justify himself, he proceeds to seek assurance:

I have been right, Basil, haven't I, to take my love out of poetry, and to find my wife in Shakespeare's plays? Lips that Shakespeare taught to speak have whispered their secret in my ear. I have had the arms of Rosalind around me, and kissed Juliet on the mouth.[15]

Hallward's response is tentative. Lord Henry, more deflationary, asks Dorian at what point he mentioned the word marriage. He proceeds to expand on the theme of Hedonism: 'When we are happy we are always good, but when we are good we are not always happy.'[16] Ominously, Lord Henry drives away to the theatre with Dorian, leaving the painter, silent and preoccupied, to follow in a hansom. The revelation which Dorian has promised his friends does not materialise. Sibyl Vane's beauty is as striking as ever, and when as Juliet she appears at her father Capulet's ball she is described in terms which seem to associate her with the perfected dancer, the human apotheosised in art, at once natural and artificial:

Her body swayed as she danced, as a plant sways in the water. The curves of her throat were the curves of a white lily. Her hands seemed to be made of cool ivory.

But the revelation promised by her physical appearance proves misleading:

The voice was exquisite, but from the point of view of tone it was absolutely false. It was wrong in colour. It took away all the life from the verse. It made the passion unreal.[17]

The process of demythologising continues: 'The staginess of her acting was unbearable . . . Her gestures became absurdly artificial . . .', until the final and laconic condemnation, 'It was simply bad art.'[18]

The audience's reactions to the performance are interestingly differentiated. Wilde, somewhat unrealistically, makes even the 'common, uneducated audience of the pit and gallery' grow restless, and eventually tramp out. Hallward attempts to reassure Dorian by separating the girl from the actress, in one of those Wildean affirmations that carry scant conviction: 'Love is a more wonderful thing than Art.' Lord Henry delivers a dandiacal truth: 'It is not good for one's morals to see bad acting.' Dorian confesses that his heart is breaking. Backstage, after the performance, Sibyl is standing 'with a look of triumph on her face':

When he entered, she looked at him, and an expression of infinite joy came over her. 'How badly I acted tonight, Dorian!' she cried.[19]

Her explanation is the most significant speech Wilde gives to her. Before she met Dorian, acting was the one reality of her life. She knew 'nothing but shadows', and thought them real. Dorian brought her 'something higher, something of which all art' was 'but a reflection'. She expected to be wonderful that night, found she could do nothing, and suddenly realised that it would be 'profanation' to 'play at being in love'.

However, just as Dorian's confession of love has stifled Sibyl's ability to act, so her withdrawal from art has killed Dorian's love: 'Without your art you are nothing.'[20] He rejects her coldly, and tells her he can never see her again. Then, in a sequence closely modelled on Lord Arthur Savile's night-walking after Podgers's prophecy of murder, Dorian wanders through the dark London underworld before dawn breaks on a Covent Garden purified by pastoral·overtones. It is on returning to his house that Dorian notices on his portrait lines of cruelty round the mouth. The next day he is full of remorse and resolves to make reparation to Sibyl:

She could still be his wife. His unreal and selfish love would yield to some higher influence, would be transformed into some nobler passion, and the portrait that Basil Hallward had painted of him would be a guide to him through life, would be to him what holiness is to some, and conscience to others, and the fear of God to us all.[21]

As he finishes a passionate letter to Sibyl, imploring her forgiveness, Lord Henry arrives with the news of Sibyl's suicide, and consoles Dorian with the idea that her lonely death was simply an episode from art, 'a strange lurid fragment from some Jacobean tragedy': 'Mourn for Ophelia, if you like. Put ashes on your head because Cordelia was strangled . . . But don't waste your tears over Sibyl Vane. She was less real than they are.' Dorian thanks Lord Henry: 'You have explained me to myself.'[22] An hour later 'and he was at the Opera, and Lord Henry was leaning over his chair'.[23]

The Sibyl Vane relationship, which effectively occupies Chapters 4 to 9, forms the crucial action within the novel. It is the test which confirms Lord Henry's domination over Dorian: in terms of the choice with which Dorian is confronted, he instinctively chooses art rather than love, confirming in practice the poisonous theories which he first heard from Lord Henry in Basil Hallward's garden. Dorian's choice is analogous to Faustus's (and Faust's) first action of egotistical self-delight; and the Mephistophelean figure of Lord Henry is present to strengthen the protagonist's resolve. Dorian's action also prompts two self-destructive revelations. The first is that of Sibyl Vane herself, whose belief in art is destroyed by the declaration of Dorian's love, love which is itself presented as essentially ephemeral, an act of imagination, as suggested by her whimsical name for Dorian of 'Prince Charming'. The second comes from Basil Hallward, who calls on Dorian the day after Lord Henry's visit and is led into confessing his secret. Hallward defines the climactic moment when he drew Dorian not as Paris, Adonis, Antinous, but in his own dress and in his own time. Before, 'it had all been what art should be, unconscious, ideal, remote',[24] but his wonderful portrait of Dorian in the method of realism would, he feared, reveal to others his idolatry. The inter-penetration of personal feeling and the artistic process is presented as fatal. Dorian translated into art is lost to Basil Hallward; Sibyl Vane, translated out of art by Dorian, is lost to him. Wilde conveys vividly the extreme fragility and tran-sitoriness of his images of perfection: the moment when the portrait is completed, which almost immediately informs Dorian of his mortality; the absorption of Sibyl Vane within her Shakespearean roles, which cannot be sustained within a context of reality. Against these exquisite but essentially tragic experiences Wilde sets the cool objectivity of Lord Henry, who remains a spectator, judging life by the standards of the connoisseur. For Dorian, once he has accepted as his mentor Lord Henry and his dictum – 'to cure the soul by means of the senses, and the senses by means of the soul' – the portrait will become the living symbol of his Faustian choice:

Eternal youth, infinite passion, pleasures subtle and secret, wild joys and wilder sins – he was to have all these things. The portrait was to bear the burden of his shame: that was all.[25]

The Sibyl Vane episode is handled more convincingly than the explanation of Basil Hallward's infatuation with Dorian, where Wilde seems, understandably, constrained by the need to suppress intimations of homosexuality. Absorption with the relationship between actress or dancer and her role is a prevalent theme in the nineteenth century, particularly since acting style became progressively more naturalistic. Wilde's choice of roles for Sibyl Vane – Juliet, Ophelia, Desdemona, Cordelia – recalls the Shakespearean characters in which Harriet Smithson appeared before Berlioz, who, like Dorian, imagined that by loving the transmitting actress he was somehow communing with Shakespeare himself. The descriptions of Sibyl as Rosalind owe something to *Mademoiselle de Maupin*, and perhaps to the open-air production of *As You Like It* produced by Lady Archibald Campbell and Godwin. There may also be an echo of Baudelaire's *La Fanfarlo*, in which the youthful Samuel Cramer, paying court to the actress in her boudoir, insists that she assume the make-up and costume of the stage role which she was portraying when he became infatuated with her, so recreating the artifice of the theatre within the context of reality.

For the extended version of *The Picture of Dorian Gray*, Wilde added a chapter (Chapter 5) which presents a number of difficulties. Its subject is Sibyl Vane and her family, her vulgarly melodramatic mother and her protective, morose brother James. The settings – their shabby lodging-house in Euston Road, the London streets, the park – have both a specificity and a shabby urban realism which contrast sharply with the decorated style which has dominated hitherto. This realism is continued in the descriptions of the tawdry theatre where Sibyl performs, and in Dorian's descent into the underworld in Chapter 16 (another addition to the original scheme). Chapter 5 is the only section in which Wilde focusses on a subject other than Dorian, who makes one brief appearance, driving past Sibyl and James as they sit in the park, but who is otherwise referred to only as Prince Charming. The change in focus is matched by an abrupt change in tone, or rather changes: the chapter contains the most uneven writing of the entire novel. In places, Wilde seems to be parodying the most banal examples of domestic melodrama:

73

Mrs Vane winced, and put her thin bismuth-whitened hands on her daughter's head. 'Happy!' she echoed, 'I am only happy, Sibyl, when I see you act. You must not think of anything but your acting. Mr Isaacs has been very good to us, and we owe him money.'
The girl looked up and pouted. 'Money, mother?' she cried. 'What does money matter? Love is more than money.'[26]

Wilde signals awareness of the effect by imputing it to Mrs Vane:

Mrs Vane glanced at her, and with one of those false theatrical gestures that so often become a mode of second nature to a stage-player, clasped her in her arms . . . a young lad with rough brown hair came into the room . . . Mrs Vane fixed her eyes on him, and intensified her smile. She mentally elevated her son to the dignity of an audience. She felt sure that the *tableau* was interesting.[27]

But in fact the melodramatic influence is pervasive, and even Sibyl's rebuke to James – 'You are like one of the heroes of those silly melodramas mother used to be so fond of acting in'[28] – does not justify or place securely the cumulative burden of derivative phrases. Wilde barely differentiates Sibyl's mode of expression from that of the rest of the family – or no more than the virtuous heroine is habitually differentiated from the rough-tongued, good-hearted brother or the vain mother. The plain and simple, unless within the artful context of a children's story, did not flow easily from Wilde. Wilde is, conceivably, presenting Sibyl's version of the romance as a fairy-tale – 'Prince Charming rules life for us now'[25] – and hence a counterpart to Dorian's equally transitory enchantment with the actress as Shakespearean heroine; but the narrative method is here too inconsistent to convey any clear structural purpose. The insertion forms a brief but disruptive interlude, compounded by its sequel, James Vane's attempted revenge and accidental death in Wilde's prefiguring of Isabel Colegate's *The Shooting Party*.

The second major episode in the novel concerns the 'poison' book, whose arrival is immediately preceded by the concealment of the picture in Dorian's former playroom. Returning to the library, Dorian finds two objects sent by Lord Henry: 'On a little table of dark perfumed wood thickly incrusted with nacre' was 'a book bound in yellow paper, the cover slightly torn and the edges soiled';[30] and, on the tea-tray, the *St James's Gazette*. In the newspaper paragraph Dorian reads of the ugly reality of Sibyl's death. Then, taking up the yellow book, he becomes absorbed:

It was the strangest book that he had ever read. It seemed to him that in exquisite raiment, and to the delicate sounds of flutes, the sins of the world were passing in dumb show before him. Things that he had dimly dreamed of were suddenly made real to him. Things of which he had never dreamed were gradually revealed.[31]

In function, the book serves a similar purpose to that of Apuleius's *Metamorphoses* in *Marius the Epicurean*, and to Ronsard's works in Pater's unfinished novel *Gaston de Latour*, which each exercised a powerful effect on the respective hero at a crucial stage of his development. (One might add the influence on Wilde himself of Pater's *The Renaissance* – 'that book which has had such a strange influence over my life'.)[32] For Dorian, however, the poison book is less a formative influence than a distraction once he has committed his self-defining act of objective cruelty towards Sibyl Vane, in something of the same way that the spectacle of the Seven Deadly Sins feeds Faustus's soul when he begins to waver. At the end of Chapter 11, Wilde summarises the novel's impact: 'Dorian Gray had been poisoned by a book. There were moments when he looked on evil simply as a mode through which he could realize his conception of the beautiful.'[33] The book confirms Dorian in evil. The consequences of his cruelty towards Sibyl Vane have been unforeseen. He now embarks upon a course of life which consciously embraces sin.

In Wilde's typescript for *Lippincott's*, the novel is called '*Le Secret de Raoul* par Catulle Sarrazin' and it would seem that Wilde at one stage planned to create an imaginary book. In the event the poison novel bears, in spite of certain discrepancies, an unmistakable resemblance to Huysmans's *A Rebours*; and Dorian shares a number of interests and enthusiasms with Huysmans's hero Des Esseintes. These interests are described by Wilde in an astonishing sequence of economical transcriptions, drawing on books he had recently reviewed, or on sources like the South Kensington Museum Handbooks for Precious Stones or Textile Fabrics. The descriptions are not particularly memorable, relying for effect on sheer cumulative weight of example, rather than on any sensory finesse in the language.

As to Dorian's sins, Wilde offers no detail. Here, indeed, as later in *De Profundis*, he appears obsessed by the word sin itself, as though its use was self-explanatory. Instead of the particularity of Huysmans – Des Esseintes's encounters with Miss Urania the American acrobat, or the ventriloquist enacting Flaubert's

Chimera and Sphinx – Wilde offers only the disconcerting tone of popular fiction:

it was said that on one occasion, when he was brought into the smoking-room of the Churchill, the Duke of Berwick and another gentleman got up in a marked manner and went out. Curious stories became current about him after he had passed his twenty-fifth year. It was rumoured that he had been seen brawling with foreign sailors in a low den in the distant parts of Whitechapel, and that he consorted with thieves and coiners and knew the mysteries of their trade.[34]

The style is reminiscent of the adventure fiction of John Buchan.

What holds the work together, here as throughout *The Picture of Dorian Gray*, is the sequence of passages which describe Dorian's relationship with his soul; the occasion when

he himself would creep upstairs to the locked room, open the door with the key that never left him now, and stand, with a mirror, in front of the portrait that Basil Hallward had painted of him, looking at the evil and ageing face on the canvas, and now at the fair young face that laughed back at him from the polished glass. The very sharpness of the contrast used to quicken his sense of pleasure. He grew more and more enamoured of his own beauty, more and more interested in the corruption of his own soul. He would examine with minute care, and sometimes with a monstrous and terrible delight, the hideous lines that seared the wrinkling forehead or crawled around the heavy sensual mouth, wondering sometimes which were the more horrible, the signs of sin or the signs of age. He would place his white hands beside the coarse bloated hands of the picture, and smile. He mocked the misshapen body and the failing limbs.[35]

This and similar passages convey a psychological conviction that validates Dorian's experiments in Hedonism, and precipitates the final crushing of conscience expressed through the murder of Basil Hallward, who calls, good angel-like, to ask Dorian if the terrible rumours he has heard about him are true. The two chapters which describe this episode, Chapters 12 and 13, contain the full range of Gothic effects: damp odour of mildewed candles, cold current of air, exclamations of horror, and finally the drip, drip of blood on threadbare carpet, and the secret press in the wainscotting. Here Wilde strikes one as being wholly in command of the idiom, using it consciously for precise effect. In the following chapter, he has Dorian stretch out on the sofa reading poems from Gautier's *Emaux et Camées* while he awaits the arrival of his scientist friend Campbell, whom he blackmails into disposing of Hallward's body. The contrast between the two frames of reference, the decadent and the Gothic, seems appropriate in both literary and psychological terms:

> When he had stretched himself on the sofa, he looked at the title-page of the book. It was Gautier's 'Emaux et Camées', Charpentier's Japanese-paper edition, with the Jacquemart etching. The binding was of citron-green leather, with a design of gilt trellis-work and dotted pomegranates. It had been given to him by Adrian Singleton. As he turned over the pages his eye fell on the poem about the hand of Lacenaire, the cold yellow hand 'du supplice encore mal lavée', with its downy red hairs and its 'doigts de faune'. He glanced at his own white taper fingers, shuddering slightly in spite of himself, and passed on . . .[36]

Lacenaire, the murderer executed by guillotine, with his 'cold yellow hand', is juxtaposed with Dorian, who has committed a comparable crime, with his white taper fingers. But even when Lacenaire is transmuted into art, the trace of reality is too disturbing, and Dorian moves on to Gautier's exquisite lines upon Venice:

> Devant une façade rose,
> Sur le marbre d'un escalier.

Dorian's memories of Venice, however, are haunted by the recollection that Basil Hallward had been with him for part of the time; and even Gautier's evocation of the Sphinx cannot distract him from the terror of what he has done.

In the novel's original scheme, the horror of the disposal of Hallward's body, and the corresponding reaction registered by the picture, an image of 'loathsome red dew that gleamed, wet and glistening, on one of the hands, as though the canvas had sweated blood', leads swiftly on to the final episode, Dorian's attempt to commit a good action, his terrible discovery that he is incapable of change and the culminating act of destruction with the knife. While the *Lippincott* version is shocking in its abruptness, the four chapters which Wilde inserted here flesh out the course of Dorian's life, intensify our sense of his suffering and clarify the persona of Lord Henry. There are two London episodes, a society dinner party at Lady Narborough's and Dorian's visit to the London underworld of dockland opium dens; and two contrasting sequences at Dorian's country house, Selby Royal, one in the conservatory, a setting for elegant conversation, and the other in the pinewoods, where James Vane is accidentally shot. Throughout these scenes there is a recurrent motif of death. While Dorian receives repeated reassurances that he is safe, both from events and from Lord Henry, the sense that he is damned becomes increasingly insistent.

These chapters contain numerous echoes of Wilde's other work. Lady Narborough seems like a preliminary sketch for Lady Hunstanton, and several of Lord Henry's conversational flourishes will be given to Lord Illingworth in *A Woman of No Importance*, while Madame de Ferrol, *décolletée* in Vienna, presages Mrs Cheveley in *An Ideal Husband*. The rhythms, and indeed some of the content, of the dialogue between Lord Henry and the Duchess of Monmouth recur in Lord Illingworth's verbal fencing with Mrs Allonby. The descriptions of the London underworld reflect similar images in 'Lord Arthur Savile's Crime' and 'The Harlot's House':

Most of the windows were dark, but now and then fantastic shadows were silhouetted against some lamp-lit blind. He watched them curiously. They moved like monstrous marionettes, and made gestures like live things.[37]

Such echoes and repetitions might be taken simply as the consequence of hasty writing; more probably, they indicate Wilde's attempts to create a satisfactory unity out of the ideas, images and styles which were his current concern. There are, too, passages which have more resonance when read in conjunction with *De Profundis*, and even *The Ballad of Reading Gaol*:

There are moments, psychologists tell us, when the passion for sin, or for what the world calls sin, so dominates a nature, that every fibre of the body, as every cell of the brain, seems to be instinct with fearful impulses. Men and women at such moments lose the freedom of their will. They move to their terrible end as automatons move. Choice is taken from them, and conscience is either killed, or, if it lives at all, lives but to give rebellion its fascination, and disobedience its charm. For all sins, as theologians weary not of reminding us, are sins of disobedience. When that high spirit, that morning-star of evil, fell from heaven, it was as a rebel that he fell.

Callous, concentrated on evil, with stained mind and soul hungry for rebellion, Dorian Gray hastened on, quickening his step as he went, but as he darted aside into a dim archway, that had served him often as a short cut to the ill-famed place where he was going, he felt himself suddenly seized from behind, and before he had time to defend himself he was thrust back against the wall, with a brutal hand round his throat.[38]

In contexts such as this, Wilde gives indications that the novel is a portrait of the artist; James Joyce detected in it 'some wish to put himself before the world'.[39]

If Wilde was intending to 'put himself before the world', he contrived to do it in a complex, multiple form. Pater, reviewing the
novel, comments that Wilde is 'impersonal: seems not to have
identified himself with any one of his characters'.[40] Wilde himself
wrote: 'Basil Hallward is what I think I am: Lord Henry what the
world thinks me: Dorian what I would like to be – in other ages,
perhaps.'[41] In Wilde's myth, Basil Hallward is killed; Dorian, an
image of perpetual youth, is spiritually dead; and Lord Henry
refuses to acknowledge the existence of the soul. Earlier on the
night of Dorian's death Lord Henry recounts to him how he heard
a London street-preacher yelling out, 'what does it profit a man
if he gain the whole world and lose – how does the quotation run?
– his own soul':

'I thought of telling the prophet that Art had a soul, but that man had
not. I am afraid, however, he would not have understood me.'
'Don't, Harry. The soul is a terrible reality. It can be bought, and sold,
and bartered away. It can be poisoned, or made perfect. There is a soul
in each one of us. I know it.'
'Do you feel quite sure of that, Dorian?'
'Quite sure.'
'Ah! then it must be an illusion. The things one feels absolutely certain
about are never true. That is the fatality of Faith, and the lesson of
Romance. How grave you are! Don't be so serious. What have you or
I to do with the superstitions of our age? No: we have given up our belief
in the soul. Play me something. Play me a nocturne, Dorian, and, as you
play, tell me, in a low voice, how you have kept your youth. You must
have some secret. I am only ten years older than you are, and I am
wrinkled, and worn, and yellow. You are really wonderful, Dorian. You
have never looked more charming than you do to-night.'[42]

The ageing Lord Henry, distancing death and divorce with
Chopin nocturnes, curing the soul by means of the sense, uses
Dorian as the corner-stone of his philosophy, the perfect
completed image:

At present you are a perfect type. Don't make yourself incomplete. You
are quite flawless now . . . I am so glad that you have never done
anything, never carved a statue, or painted a picture, or produced
anything outside of yourself! Life has been your art. You have set yourself
to music. Your days are your sonnets.[43]

It is significant that Wilde places the emphasis throughout the
penultimate chapter on Lord Henry, while Dorian is shown
retreating more and more into his renunciation of sin, and
his resolution to be good. Lord Henry's affirmations become

increasingly declamatory as the scene reaches its close – 'Art has no influence upon action. It annihilates the desire to act. It is superbly sterile'[44] – echoing the Preface which Wilde attached to the revised work. As Dorian leaves, he hesitates for a moment, 'as if he had something more to say. Then he sighed and went out'.[45] The work's final image, the dead man 'withered, wrinkled, and loathsome of visage', recognisable only by his rings, is set against the previous chapter's farewell, and the plan to ride in the park to see the lilacs. It is a pattern which Wilde will further refine in *Salomé*.

6

Plays: the social comedies

Wilde's first public success as a playwright came with *Lady Windermere's Fan*, written during the early autumn of 1891 at the instigation of the actor–manager George Alexander. It is sometimes suggested that this social comedy and its successors, *A Woman of No Importance* and *An Ideal Husband*, are of relatively slight significance, trifles tossed off by Wilde for purely commercial considerations and modelled, tongue in cheek, upon contemporary patterns with the intention of both flattering and mocking their fashionable audiences. John Russell Taylor's judgment, that 'Wilde does not give the impression, even for a moment, that he takes all this nonsense seriously. The plots are creaking old contrivances . . .'[1] is representative of such a view; and statements like Ada Leverson's, that 'in truth he cared little for any of his plays excepting only *Salomé*',[2] lend support to it.

Wilde frequently adopted an attitude of insouciance towards his work for the theatre – when he was not justifying it fiercely. To Lady Bancroft's comment that the leading situation in one of his comedies reminded her of a scene in a play by Scribe, Wilde 'unblushingly replied: "Taken bodily from it, dear lady. Why not? Nobody reads nowadays."'[3] In response to Beerbohm Tree's praise for the plot of *A Woman of No Importance*, Wilde claimed that 'Plots are tedious. Anyone can invent them. Life is full of them . . . I took the plot of this play from *The Family Herald*, which took it – wisely, I feel, from my novel *The Picture of Dorian Gray*.'[4] That explanation seems an appropriately Wildean conjunction of life and art. Contrarily, in connection with *An Ideal Husband*, he wrote: 'I have been considerably amused by so many of the critics suggesting that the incident of the diamond bracelet in Act 3 of my new play was suggested by Sardou. It does not occur in any of Sardou's plays, and it was not in my play until less than ten days before production. Nobody else's work gives me any suggestion.'[5]

There are many examples of similar disclaimers. Wilde was, in fact, infinitely suggestible, but also endlessly inventive when he wished to be. The plots of his plays were less important to him than the language. Yet it would be wrong to assume any indifference to stage-technique. His detailed stage-directions and settings, the close interest he maintained in rehearsals, the well-known disagreement with Alexander about the curtain-line for Act Two of *Lady Windermere's Fan*, all indicate that he was fully as concerned about and sensitive to the more mechanical aspects of stage-craft as he was, unsurprisingly, to the visual and verbal conveyance of manner and form.

Wilde's early plays are *Vera, or the Nihilists*, published in 1880 and produced in New York in August 1883, where it ran for a week; and *The Duchess of Padua*, written during 1883 but first presented (as *Guido Ferranti*) again in New York for a brief season in 1891. *Vera* is a somewhat superficial and excessively melodramatic treatment of Nihilism set in contemporary Russia. The play was actually in rehearsal at the Adelphi Theatre with Mrs Bernard Beere in the title role when it was withdrawn in November 1881, ostensibly because of 'the present state of political feeling in England'. Since the Czar, Alexander II, had been assassinated in March 1881, the central event of Wilde's play written the previous year, there were some grounds for such a postponement. Until *An Ideal Husband* and *The Ballad of Reading Gaol*, Wilde never again treated contemporary material so directly. The play, for all its rawness, has much of interest, particularly in the bold, near-symbolic deployment of costume and stage-setting. With the character of Vera, Wilde places a sympathetic, non-conforming woman in the central role. Prince Paul, his flippancy startlingly tangential to the melodrama that surrounds him, anticipates the role of the dandy in Wilde's later comedies, and is the mouthpiece for a number of epigrams Wilde thought too good to abandon. *Vera* was, if nothing else, a useful training exercise. As Symons commented, 'All actors should be sent to school in melodrama as all dramatic authors should learn their trade there.'[6]

The Duchess of Padua is adroit pastiche, a revenge verse-drama by Hugo out of Shakespeare and Webster, and strongly reminiscent of Shelley's *The Cenci*. It is described minutely by Wilde in a long letter to the actress Mary Anderson, for whom he intended the title role: the detailed analysis of scenery and costume reveals Wilde's acute sensitivity to the visual dimension in this and all his plays.[7] *The Duchess of Padua* has little in common with the social comedies, though there are some interesting reverse-image contrasts between Guido and Beatrice, and Sir Robert and Lady Chiltern. Less specifically, work on these plays provided Wilde with essential practical experience. If one adds an innate sense of the dramatic, and the close knowledge of contemporary theatre which he acquired through extensive and critical playgoing and professional intimacy with actors and actresses, there were substantial foundations upon which Wilde could construct his own distinctive kind of drama. That he contrived to make his success appear so casually achieved was part of his skill.

Lady Windermere's Fan opened at the St James's Theatre on Saturday, 20 February 1892. Alexander exerted a telling influence upon the acting text. It was at his insistence that Wilde wrote a new curtain-line for Act Two, so that the act closed not with the more traditional 'strong' speech of Mrs Erlynne, with its stress on suspense and plot:

Remember you are to keep Windermere at your club, and don't let him come back tonight.

but with the lower-key, throwaway 'character' line of Lord Augustus:

Well, really, I might be her husband already. Positively I might.
[Follows her in a bewildered manner.[8]

This alteration, slight enough in itself, indicates the general direction in which Wilde would eventually aim of his own volition: away from the emphasis on plot and contrivance, the legacy from melodrama and the well-made French *boulevard* play which still dominated the London stage, towards a reliance on gradations and cadences of language to convey character and mood.

Wilde's involvement at the rehearsal phase refutes any judgment that he was indifferent to the perfecting of his comedies. His letters to Alexander reveal both the understandable tensions between author and director, and his perception that every detail, of setting, costume, gesture, language and vocal nuance had significance for the total effect: 'Details in life are of no importance, but in art details are vital.'[9] Some of these details arose because of the play's reflection of contemporary manners. Wilde, like Bulwer Lytton in his suggestions to Macready for the first production of *Money*, was anxious that his imitation of life should be flawlessly accurate in terms of surface:

I think also that C. Graham should not take his aunt into the ballroom – young dandies dislike their aged relatives – at least rarely pay them attention. Lady J. should have a debutante in tow, and Mrs Erlynne might give the speech about Dumby to Graham, and then turn to you.

With regard to yourself, when Cecil Graham bores you with his chatter you broke off last night by saying 'How amusing!', or some word like that. I think it would be better to say 'Excuse me for a moment', as I suggested. Lord W. is terribly agitated about Mrs Erlynne's coming, and the dandy's chatter bores him, does not please him. He has no taste for it.[10]

The influence and theatrical instincts of Alexander were invaluable to Wilde. One crucial instance was his advice that the fact of Mrs Erlynne being Lady Windermere's mother should be revealed early in the play, rather than held back until Act Four as Wilde originally planned. '. . . I am bound to state that all my friends, without exception, were of opinion that the psychological interest of the second act would be greatly increased by the disclosure of the actual relationship existing between Lady Windermere and Mrs Erlynne – an opinion, I may add, that had previously been strongly held and urged by Mr Alexander.'[11] This adjustment was made on the fourth or fifth night. Although no prompt script has been located, it is almost certain that the acting version differed considerably from the text published by Wilde in 1893, in which many of the individual speeches have been expanded, when compared with the autograph draft in the British Library or the typescript in the University of Texas. The greater economy and control of the earlier texts is strikingly superior.

The play, in four acts with three settings, is concerned with a crisis in Lady Windermere's life on the day of her twenty-first birthday. Act One: Lady Windermere, a Puritan with a simple concept of good and bad, learns that her husband is paying attentions, and large sums of money, to a Mrs Erlynne, a woman 'with a past before her'. She also receives an intimation of love from Lord Darlington. Lord Windermere insists on inviting Mrs Erlynne to the dance that evening; Lady Windermere vows to strike her with her fan should she come. Act Two: Mrs Erlynne comes, but is not struck. Lord Darlington declares his love for Lady Windermere. Mrs Erlynne extracts a marriage settlement from Lord Windermere to enable her to secure Lord Augustus Lorton. Lady Windermere writes to her husband announcing her intention of leaving him. Mrs Erlynne intercepts the letter. Act Three: Lady Windermere, alone in Darlington's rooms, is about to return to her husband and child when Mrs Erlynne arrives, intent on saving her daughter from her act of folly. The whole troop of male characters enters. They discourse on the relationship between the sexes while the women remain concealed. Lady Windermere's fan is discovered. To protect her daughter's reputation Mrs Erlynne risks compromising herself in perpetuity by emerging to state that she has brought the fan herself in error, so creating a diversion that allows Lady Windermere to escape. Act Four: Lady Windermere does not explain to her husband that she was tempted by Lord Darlington. Lord Windermere does not explain to his wife that he has been blackmailed by her mother. Mrs Erlynne contrives to explain her bizarre conduct to Lord Augustus, but off-stage and by an untruth. She does not reveal to Lady Windermere that she is her mother. She leaves, with the fan, to live with Lord Augustus entirely out of England. Lady Windermere plans a retreat to the garden of their country house at Selby. For her, now thoroughly come of age, Mrs Erlynne is 'a very good woman'.

This simplified account of the story, clearly an inadequate reading of the play, is intended to emphasise one essential feature: the plot is most remarkable for what does not happen. The potentially sensational revelations of Act Four do not take place. The truth is imparted to the audience, but only partially to the characters. Such a method is closer to Ibsen than to Dumas *fils*, and Wilde repeatedly avoids the obvious theatrical gesture. At the close of Act One Lady Windermere announces, holding her birthday fan, 'If that woman crosses my threshold, I shall strike her across the face with it.' The expectation is underlined for the audience when she orders her butler, Parker, 'Be sure you pronounce the names of the guests very distinctly tonight. Sometimes you speak so fast that I miss them. I am particularly anxious to hear the names quite clearly, so as to make no mistake.' After Parker has left, Wilde gives Lady Windermere yet another speech to repeat her threat. But when Mrs Erlynne enters the Windermeres' drawing-room in Act Two, Lady Windermere merely bows coldly and walks away with Lord Darlington.

This pattern of anticipation followed by frustration recurs throughout the play. Lady Windermere goes to Lord Darlington's bachelor rooms, but has already announced that she will return to her husband by the time Mrs Erlynne arrives to persuade her. The discovery of Lady Windermere's fan by Cecil Graham, and Windermere's fustian threat to Darlington:

You scoundrel! I'll not leave your rooms till I have searched every corner of it! What moves behind that curtain?[12]

leads, not to the moral outrage and duel which the revelation of Lady Windermere's presence would bring, but to the anti-climax of Mrs Erlynne's entrance, received with contempt and knowing smiles. Act Four does not end with revelations, but ushers in a new dispensation of compromise and concealment. Here Wilde is rejecting any blatant imitation of a particular theatrical (and moral) tradition, and constructing a more playful and infinitely more subtle variation upon familiar themes and patterns.

A second feature of the plot is the way it recalls both the social dramas of Sardou and Dumas *fils* and, less insistently but more pervasively, the situations, issues and devices of Restoration comedy. Wilde was clearly at pains to give *Lady Windermere's Fan* a contemporary feel. 'Modern' is the key word in all his comedies, and the external trappings of modern life – telegrams, photographs, whisky and soda, the Club Train – are much in evidence, as are topical subjects of conversation like the Married Women's Property Act. Any suggestion that the criteria of social acceptance and its counterparts of blackmail and scandal are exaggerated or artificial may be rapidly dispelled by a glance at the facts surrounding Wilde's trials. Nevertheless, the organisation and themes of the comedies belong to a traditon which stretches back, by way perhaps of Boucicault's *London Assurance*, to Sheridan, and before him to Congreve, Vanbrugh and Etherege. The relationships between the sexes, the problems of reconciling private with public morality, love with marriage (and property), the conflict between wit and sentiment – these carry the flavour of the Restoration as surely as does the apparatus of intercepted letters, well- or ill-intentioned gossip, discovered objects and concealments behind curtains. The ubiquitous fan, relic of Restoration sexuality, itself flaunts the connection by appearing in all four acts. The discovery scene in Act Three recalls the screen scene in *The School for Scandal*, as does the chorus of scandalmongers itself. In the urbane polish and poetic balance of his dialogue, equally, Wilde resembles Sheridan and Congreve.

It should not be supposed that Wilde is attempting to imitate any one genre rather than another; however, the individual kind of comedy which he initiated and developed has even stronger affinities with the English than with the French tradition. One striking principle of construction in *Lady Windermere's Fan*, which corroborates such a view, is the way in which it is organised, in part, by means of a hierarchy of wit. Such a scheme would place Mrs Erlynne and Lord Darlington in the highest rank, their tone being echoed by an essentially choric voice like Cecil Graham's; and the apparently witless Lord Augustus at the bottom. By matching Mrs Erlynne and Lord Augustus, Wilde achieves a surprising and ironic effect of reversal at the play's close. Lord Darlington, however, presents a more intractable dramatic problem when he ceases to function as a dandiacal commentator and assumes the role of a solemn and somewhat puritanical lover. Unlike Shakespeare with Benedick, Wilde here proves incapable of controlling a witty lover who is converted to seriousness. The Darlington who corrects Lady Windermere in Act One:

It is absurd to divide people into good and bad. People are either charming or tedious.[13]

risks becoming either tedious or ludicrous himself when he declares in Act Two:

This is the last time I shall ever look on you. You will never see me again. For one moment our lives met – our souls touched. They must never meet or touch again. Good-bye, Margaret.[14]

Throughout the badinage of the men's chorus in Act Three Darlington remains serious and sincere: 'No, we are all in the gutter, but some of us are looking at the stars.' The role of Wildean commentator also falls partly upon Cecil Graham, but Graham never rises above cynicism. The silencing of Lord Darlington, and his absence from Act Four, alter the balance of the play; Wilde has left himself only Mrs Erlynne to maintain the dandy's point of view, and the absence of any intellectual foil restricts her impact.

The difficulty of placing the dandy satisfactorily within the dramatic context remained Wilde's most intractable aesthetic problem: it is the problem of 'finding a world fit for the dandy to live in'. As Ian Gregor has observed, 'like the tramp, who was to succeed him in the mythology of a later drama, the dandy is a displaced person . . .'[15] The dandy, like the Shakespearean fool, or a Jaques or a Lucio, functions most effectively as commentator when unassimilated into, or at least distanced from, the action. Darlington abandons form for feeling; Cecil Graham is mere mask, with no feeling to conceal. Mrs Erlynne, sustainer of the dandiacal and so of the Wildean perspective, is compelled to abandon England and live abroad in self-imposed exile. The dandiacal world which Wilde has lightly sketched is shown to be irreconcilable with the milieu of philistine London society. The choices appear to be threefold. The first is to fulfil the outward forms of convention but to flout them whenever convenient or possible; this is what, in different ways, the Duchess of Berwick, Lady Plymdale, and Cecil Graham do – and in this hierarchy Graham is the chief, since he is the most consciously witty and cynical:

Now, I never moralize. A man who moralizes is usually a hypocrite, a woman who moralizes is invariably plain.[16]

The second choice is to escape abroad, like Darlington and Mrs Erlynne; as Mrs Erlynne says,

London is too full of fogs and serious people, Lord Windermere. Whether the fogs produce the serious people or whether the serious people produce the fogs, I don't know, but the whole thing rather gets on my nerves, and so I'm leaving this afternoon by the Club Train.[17]

The third course is also a retreat, this time to the rose-garden at Selby where the roses are white and red. The play closes on this double note of departure, and on the moral ambiguity of the Windermeres' statements – the ambiguity intensified by their recipient, the lackwit Lord Augustus:

LORD WINDERMERE: Well, you are certainly marrying a very clever woman!
LADY WINDERMERE [*taking her husband's hand*]: Ah, you're marrying a very good woman![18]

Lord Windermere's comment recognises, even if he does not, Mrs Erlynne's dandiacal quality of mastering life: she has acquired wealth, a title and a husband from her foray within the London season. Lady Windermere's tribute both places Mrs Erlynne for the audience – the sub-title is 'A play about a good woman' – and reflects upon her own coming-of-age gift, the ability to make a new and better kind of moral judgment to replace those she learned from her stern Aunt Julia:

she taught me what the world is forgetting, the difference that there is between what is right and what is wrong. *She* allowed of no compromise. *I* allow of none.[19]

Now she understands that

There is the same world for all of us, and good and evil, sin and innocence, go through it hand in hand.[20]

That final insight is one of a number of indications that Lady Windermere is her mother's daughter, impulsive, passionate, capable of moral and intellectual development. She is matched, however, with a pompous and ponderous man who seems rather to regress towards Aunt Julia's moral code; in the last act, his speeches are full of phrases like 'a bad woman preying upon life', 'worthless, vicious', 'you fill me with horror'. By the side of Lord Windermere, Lord Augustus Lorton appears a more reasonable proposition.

The most important elements of the play's organisation are the hierarchy of wit; the gifts presented to Lady Windermere on her coming of age (themselves arranged in an ascending hierarchy, from the fan to love and finally wisdom); and the retreat from London society to the country, which is also a retreat from sexual temptation to the natural obligations of motherhood. Here the three elements merge, as the witty Mrs Erlynne removes the fan, symbol of coquetry, and Lady Windermere is released to the idea of the rose-garden, the symbol of natural innocence which began the sequence: at the play's opening, Lady Windermere receives Lord Darlington while arranging the roses from Selby, a symbolic action which continues as he examines her birthday fan. All three elements, too, combine to act as implicit satirical comment on the hypocrisy of English upper-class society. The strand of satire is present in each of Wilde's comedies, though seldom intrusive.

Society, and its London centrepiece the season, is depicted as a sexual market-place. There are three major sexual encounters surrounding the Windermeres' marriage: Lord Darlington's pursuit of Lady Windermere (justified on the grounds that Windermere has broken the bonds of marriage and so set her free, though Windermere's interest in Mrs Erlynne is not, of course, what it seems); Mrs Erlynne's pursuit of Lord Augustus; and Lady Agatha's mother-directed quest for Mr Hopper. These three encounters are placed in the glittering context of the Windermeres' 'small and early' dance, and the superficiality of the values which inform such functions is both implicitly and explicitly exposed. There are light economic vignettes, such as the ingratiating Dumby, whose prototype was presumably applauding from the stalls:

DUMBY: Good evening, Lady Stutfield. I suppose this will be the last ball of the season?
LADY STUTFIELD: I suppose so, Mr Dumby. It's been a delightful season, hasn't it?
DUMBY: Quite delightful! Good evening, Duchess. I suppose this will be the last ball of the season?
DUCHESS OF BERWICK: I suppose so, Mr Dumby. It has been a very dull season, hasn't it?
DUMBY: Dreadfully dull! Dreadfully dull!
MRS COWPER-COWPER: Good evening, Mr Dumby. I suppose this will be the last ball of the season?
DUMBY: Oh I think not. There'll probably be two more.[21]

More pointedly, there is the Duchess of Berwick's campaign to marry her complaisant daughter Lady Agatha to the wealthy Australian – 'Ah, we know your value, Mr Hopper. We wish there were more like you' – which is satisfactorily accomplished by the end of the ball, and which serves as an echo of the maturer hunting of Lord Augustus by Mrs Erlynne and also, perhaps, of the earlier match between the Windermeres. The most telling critiques are those which are only implied: for instance, Mrs Erlynne's ability to blackmail Lord Windermere because of the shock which the truth might give to her daughter. Reminiscent in places of the fairy-stories, the comedies develop their own kind of oblique moral commentary. A world which must have seemed delightfully familiar to its fashionable audience is progressively undermined.

In terms of act and scene structure, the play is tightly controlled. The roses of the opening, and the image of the country garden at the close, provide the natural framework for the two private, though formal, morning-room scenes of Act One and Act Four. At the centre stand juxtaposed the large-scale scenes: the ball, with band playing, banks of flowers and brilliant lights, in which the women are in the forefront; and the more sombre setting of Lord Darlington's rooms, the male preserve, where the latent hostility to women expressed in the brittle, heartless conversation of Dumby and Graham is reinforced by the contrast between their dark formal clothes and the isolation of the beautifully dressed Mrs Erlynne. It is social death not to be seen with a man at the first, and social infamy to be found with a man in the second. The visual dimension is as important in these comedies as in *Salomé*, and not just in terms of delight, though 'a play about society people by Oscar Wilde was inevitably a dress parade'.[22] Lady Windermere's growth from innocence to maturity of judgment is partly conveyed by such contrasts as that between the opening image as she stands, her hands wet, to arrange the roses, and her exhaustion as she lies on the sofa at the beginning of Act Four; or when her refusal to shake hands with Lord Darlington in the opening sequence is recalled by the play's last gesture as she takes her husband's hand.

Any opening night of a play by Oscar Wilde was itself a dramatic event. His name and reputation were sufficient to secure attention; but he was also the first major English literary figure to write a comedy for years. His ostentatious presence increased the sense of occasion. Wilde's response to the audience's call for the author is notorious: smoking a cigarette (interpreted by many as a deliberate insult), he addressed them in a manner which anticipates Archie Rice in *The Entertainer*: 'I congratulate you on the *great* sense of your performance, which persuades me that you think almost as highly of the play as I do myself.' It is not surprising that the critics, whom Wilde held in even greater contempt than most playwrights do, found it hard to decide how seriously to take play or author. The enigmatic critical response matched the ambiguity of the play's own conclusion. The play's apparent clash between the rhythms and tone of ironic comedy and those of melodrama can be overcome in performance, and are far less obtrusive if viewed in a context which includes, for instance, Ibsen and Chekhov. Behind Mrs Erlynne may lie Mrs Alving, from *Ghosts*, or Hedda Gabler, whose portrayal by Elizabeth Robins the previous year had so impressed Wilde. Katharine Worth has argued that

Brack's famous phrase 'People don't do such things' is surely recalled in Mrs Erlynne's mocking 'I suppose, Windermere, you would like me to retire into a convent, or become a hospital nurse . . . That is stupid of you, Arthur; in real life we don't do such things'; Mrs Erlynne and Hedda Gabler are in a similarly ironical and critical relationship to a society obsessed with surface respectability.[23]

The interest of Wilde's first comedy lies in his capacity to suggest, through the rhythms and patterns of the dramatic texture, what lies beneath the surface, both of the society he evokes and of the characters he creates.

The writing of *Salomé*, and abortive rehearsals for a first production frustrated by the Lord Chamberlain, intervened before Wilde began to construct his next social comedy, *A Woman of No Importance*. This play, like the other comedies, reflects (in the name of Lady Hunstanton) the part of England where Wilde wrote the first draft, in this instance Norfolk. The play was written for Beerbohm Tree, for whom Wilde conceived the role of Lord Illingworth, and produced by him, 'with interference' from the author, at the Theatre Royal, Haymarket on 19 April 1893.

Wilde chose, as contrast to the London season setting of *Lady Windermere's Fan*, an English country house-party. Again, he uses as the central situation the woman with a secret past, though the emphasis is here shifted to Mrs Arbuthnot's encounter with her former lover, now Lord Illingworth, and her son's discovery of and reaction to the truth about their relationship. In place of an

Australian heir to a fruit-canning fortune, he deploys an orphaned American heiress to a dry-goods empire, Hester Worsley, who combines the function of serious lover with that of moral commentator and exposer of English hypocrisy. Her counterpart is the illegitimate Gerald Arbuthnot, about to be rescued from provincial obscurity and boredom by the patronage of his unsuspecting father. The roles of dandy are given to Mrs Allonby and, more crucially, to Lord Illingworth. This creates an aesthetic problem for Wilde, since Lord Illingworth, in terms of plot, is also the villain. The rest of the dramatis personae are a sparkling collection of grotesques and fools, who comprise a more varied range than that in *Lady Windermere's Fan*. Two serve as shadowy forerunners for the perfected models of *The Importance of Being Earnest*: the Archdeacon, miraculously calm in the face of his absent wife's multiple illnesses, bears a trace of Chasuble; while the elderly Lady Hunstanton, unusually benevolent for a Wilde character, anticipates Lady Bracknell in her imperfect grasp of fact and in the erratic conjunction of the naive and the worldly in her analysis of social behaviour. The rest pass in and out of view, endlessly though vainly pursuing each other; the lovely but brainless Lady Stutfield, eager for flirtation; Sir John Pontefract, anxious to oblige; the acidic Lady Caroline Pontefract, tracking her husband through the music-room and terrace; the heavily married Mr Kelvil in search of an audience for his discourses on Purity or Bimetallism. These minor characters, decorative or grotesque, form a diverting background to the play's main concerns. They do not properly compensate for Wilde's awkward handling of the central story.

Structurally, the play moves between two gardens. In Act One, it is a garden that, initially, epitomises England: the formal lawns and terrace of an English country house, dominated by a large yew tree. Wilde draws attention to the symbolism at the close of the act:

LORD ILLINGWORTH: Yes, let us stay here. The Book of Life begins with a man and a woman in a garden.
MRS ALLONBY: It ends with Revelations.[24]

Mrs Allonby enjoys the forms of flirtation without the outcome: the reward of the Ideal Man, she tells Lady Caroline and Lady Stutfield, is 'infinite expectation'; 'one should never surrender', and certainly not to the Ideal Man, 'unless, of course, one wants to grow tired of him'. She tempts Lord Illingworth to kiss the Puritan Miss Worsley:

LORD ILLINGWORTH: What do you think she'd do if I kissed her?
MRS ALLONBY: Either marry you, or strike you across the face with her
glove . . .[25]

It is this challenge which launches such action as there is in the
rest of the play – Wilde referred to Act One as the perfect act,
since it contained 'absolutely no action at all'. The kissing of Miss
Worsley repeats a pattern established in the past, as Lord
Illingworth later reminds Mrs Arbuthnot, 'when the whole thing
began in your father's garden'. At the close of Act Three Lord
Illingworth undertakes the experiment, thereby unleashing
Gerald's protective fury. The direct result is to reveal that Gerald
is his own son, and to transfer Gerald's sympathies back to his
mother. In Act Four, Lord Illingworth, under pressure from
Gerald, offers to marry Mrs Arbuthnot. He is rejected and, when
he insults her, is struck across the face with his own glove. In the
act's final image mother, son and daughter-in-law-to-be move
away from the world of the open lawns of the English country
house towards the refuge of Mrs Arbuthnot's secret garden.
Gerald picks up the fallen glove, symbol of a corrupt society. Mrs
Arbuthnot, unconsciously echoing Lord Illingworth's own
dismissal of her memory at the close of Act One, is able to reply
to Gerald's enquiry as to who her visitor was:

Oh! no one. No one in particular. A man of no importance.[26]

The play's scenario is not unlike that of a fairy-story. The myth
begins in the great house, or palace, where the master, in terms
of wealth and power, is Lord Illingworth, the wicked lord. He
offers gifts of various kinds to the hero Gerald (the prince in
disguise) and, at the prompting of Mrs Allonby (the malicious
witch), pretends to woo the Puritan in white muslin, the beautiful
though humble heroine. But these offers are rejected because of
the lord's wickedness, and the hero and heroine choose instead the
poor but honest cottage outside the palace gates. To a certain
degree this traditional format, which the fairy-story shares with
many melodramas, carries some consistency and conviction. It is
possible to divide the play's characters into the aristocratic (Lord
Illingworth, Mrs Allonby, the Pontefracts, Lady Hunstanton) and
the non-aristocratic (Mrs Arbuthnot, Gerald, Hester, perhaps Mr
Kelvil), and to see the play function as a dismissal of the former
and an assertion of the intrinsic value of the so-called 'unimpor-
tant'. There are other indications, besides the treatment meted
out to Lord Illingworth, which support such a reading. Two more

aristocratic characters, Lady Hunstanton and Mrs Allonby, visit the cottage in Act Four and are dismissed without seeing Mrs Arbuthnot. The judgment of Lady Hunstanton, the most neutral of the aristocrats, carries weight:

> Mrs Arbuthnot doesn't know anything about the wicked society in which we all live. She won't go into it. She is far too good. I consider it was a great honour her coming to me last night. It gave quite an atmosphere of respectability to the party.[27]

However, Mrs Allonby's reply 'Ah, that must have been what you thought was thunder in the air' works in two ways. It reminds us of the moral gulf between the two worlds; but it also emphasises that wit and elegance, and enjoyment, belong to the world of the aristocrat, or at least to that of the dandy. Mrs Arbuthnot's 'atmosphere of respectability' is associated with good works in the parish and sermons heavy with biblical allusion on the unalluring subjects of sin and maternal devotion. In terms of wit, naturally, the dandies hold the monopoly. But Wilde has also endowed them with a disproportionate share of insight, so that an audience is often faced with a choice between the kind of sensibility expressed by Gerald, which reflects his mother's education of him:

> Lord Illingworth, you have insulted the purest thing on God's earth, a thing as pure as my own mother. You have insulted the woman I love most in the world with my own mother. As there is a God in Heaven, I will kill you![28]

and that of his father, Lord Illingworth:

> I was on the point of explaining to Gerald that the world has always laughed at its own tragedies, that being the only way in which it has been able to bear them. And that, consequently, whatever the world has treated seriously belongs to the comedy side of things.[29]

In his plays, Wilde is habitually more convincing when expressing himself through the comic than through the serious. Mrs Erlynne retains her authority because she retains her wit. Mrs Arbuthnot, for all the moral strength of her decisions in Act Four, lacks that dramatic authority which Wilde can only impart by his gift of language. That was a gift which did not extend to the sermon, as Mrs Arbuthnot's speech in Act Four demonstrates. The irony of Lord Illingworth's punishment is insufficiently supported by irony of language.

There is, too, a strange sub-text to the play, as though it is an exploration of that long-ago, forbidden sexual encounter in the garden which took place between moral, intellectual, even social opposites. The love between Gerald and Hester Worsley resembles that between siblings; the flirtations of Mrs Allonby are, by her own admission, unconsummated. The central sexual act, however, which brought Gerald into the world, resulted in sin and hatred. In *Into the Demon Universe*, Christopher Nassaar suggests that the play has a demonic content, and describes it as 'the only comedy the decadent movement ever produced'.[30] This may be claiming too much, but certainly there are pervasive symbolic undertones which stress the play's sexual dimension. These undertones are conveyed partly by the physical settings, partly by emphasis on clothing (shawls, cloaks, veil, and most significantly the glove), and partly by the patterns of movement and conversation among guests. Sex, in fact, is seen to be the ever-interesting topic, whether eagerly promoted by the aristocrats (Sir John Pontefract discoursing to Mrs Allonby on the excessively advanced views of the savages in Patagonia) or pursued in its contrary form by the Puritans like the fertile Kelvil. The dandies, Mrs Allonby and Lord Illingworth, treat sex as a game or pastime; and it is they who seem to possess Wilde's implicit approval. Mrs Arbuthnot with her foundling children is condemned to a life abroad. In England, however, 'The future belongs to the dandy. It is the exquisites who are going to rule.' *A Woman of No Importance* lacks the ironies of its predecessor, and indeed of its successor, *An Ideal Husband*. The moral statement which plot and dialogue seem to be making through the earnest characters is uneasily qualified by the vitality of the truth implied through the apparently comic and trivial.

At certain points in the play, Wilde achieves what seems to be a satisfactory state of tension between the two philosophies, or moralities. One is in Mrs Arbuthnot's final, ironic dismissal of Lord Illingworth as 'a man of no importance'; another is the scene between the two at the end of Act Two, which Archer praised as 'the most virile and intelligent . . . piece of English dramatic writing of our day . . . The interest of the scene arises from emotion based upon thought, thought thrilled with emotion. There is nothing conventional in it, nothing insincere. In a word, it is a piece of adult art.'[31] But Archer was also quick to seize on Wilde's unsubtle reliance on the conventional, contrasting the strong and simple conclusion of Act Two with the 'He is your Father!' tableau at the end of Act Three:

95

It would be a just retribution if Mr Wilde were presently to be confronted with this tableau in all the horrors of chromolithography, on every hoarding in London, with the legend, 'Stay, Gerald! He is your father!' in crinkly letters in the corner.[32]

The fustian language and gestures echo back beyond Sardou and Dumas to the great source of melodrama, Pixérécourt. A similar incursion of the language and conventions of melodrama occurs in *The Picture of Dorian Gray*, though it is less disabling because narrated. Lord Henry Wotton has many features in common with Lord Illingworth; but in the novel Wilde indicates a moral and intellectual complexity which the conventional postures and flat language – 'the spectres and shadows of the stage' – of too many of the play's sequences preclude.

Wilde's next play of modern life, *An Ideal Husband*, was presented at the Theatre Royal, Haymarket on 3 January 1895. The play, intended originally for John Hare but rejected by him, was produced by Lewis Waller with himself as Sir Robert Chiltern, Charles Hawtrey as Lord Goring, Julia Neilson (the original Hester Worsley) as Lady Chiltern and Florence West as Mrs Cheveley. The guilty secret which in the previous two plays had been sexual and focussed on a woman is here concerned with money and politics and centred upon a man. In place of the drawing-rooms and country houses of the aristocracy at leisure, Wilde has moved towards the world of public affairs, of speeches in Parliament and visits to Downing Street. In physical setting and construction, the play is once again spacious and extravagant, with three settings in the four acts. The first is especially demanding: the octagon room of Sir Robert Chiltern's house in Grosvenor Square, 'brilliantly lighted and full of guests'. Lady Chiltern stands at the *top* of the staircase to receive her guests; over the staircase well hangs a large eighteenth-century French tapestry representing, no doubt ironically at first, the Triumph of Love, from a design by Boucher. The sound of a string quartet, faintly heard, comes from the music room. The opening dialogue is given to two of those minor characters whom Wilde deploys so skilfully to create a tone and mood: two very pretty women, seated on a Louis Seize sofa, 'types of exquisite fragility' whom Watteau would have loved to paint. The emphasis on external and opulent appearance is already marked. During this overture Lady Basildon surveys the room (and presumably the auditorium, containing on the glittering first night the Prince of Wales) and remarks:

I don't see anybody here tonight whom one could possibly call a serious purpose.[33]

Wilde's ability to flatter by imitation and to mock the world he shared with his audience is especially apparent in this first act. Shaw commented on the 'subtle and pervading levity' in *An Ideal Husband* and suggested that it was a play with no thesis but 'in the purest integrity, a play and nothing less'. The extent to which Wilde was consciously playing with the plot and the characters, with dramatic form and with his audience is more noticeable in this third social comedy than in its predecessors.

The plot, more substantial than in the previous two plays yet still slight enough, centres upon Sir Robert Chiltern's guilty secret. The wealth so alluringly displayed at the reception was acquired by an act of fraud, an example of Victorian insider dealing. As a well-born but poor young man, he passed confidential information about a Government transaction to the foreign financier Baron Arnheim. (The incident bears some relation to Disraeli's handling of the Suez Canal transactions.) Mrs Cheveley, armed with a compromising letter, arrives from Vienna to blackmail Chiltern into giving public support for a suspect financial venture which will make a fortune for herself and her friends. Chiltern, who seems fated to acquiesce in order to preserve his career, and so lose his wife's trust, is rescued fortuitously by Lord Goring, who extracts the damaging letter from Mrs Cheveley by threatening her in her turn with public infamy. The puritanical Lady Chiltern is about to demand that her husband retire from public life, but Lord Goring persuades her to be more tolerant and forgiving. The play ends with a seat in the Cabinet for Sir Robert and the affirmation that a new life is beginning.

The moral scheme of the plot has, demonstrably, some unusual implications. These reflect the tolerance and compromise of *Lady Windermere's Fan* rather than the moral absolutes of *A Woman of No Importance*. The man who sold confidential information may look forward to the prospect of becoming Prime Minister; Lady Chiltern, like Lady Windermere, learns to accept a less puritanical code, though Wilde ensures that her expression of it has an ironical gloss by making her repeat the lesson she has learned from Lord Goring like a parrot:

A man's life is of more value than a woman's. It has larger issues, wider scope, greater ambitions. Our lives revolve in curves of emotions. It is upon lines of intellect that a man's life progresses.[35]

(How much of this kind of precept Wilde appproved is open to question.) Mrs Cheveley, who steals letters and diamond brooches instead of confidential information, slides through the first three acts like a reincarnation of Milady de Winter before fading from the scene, unredeemed but unpunished.

This uneven distribution of rewards and punishments, which might be considered either cynical or inelegant, is in fact held in perspective by the actions of Lord Goring, by some way the most interesting and vital character in the play. Lord Goring stands at the apex of the hierarchy of wit. He represents the dandiacal point of view; he functions as Wildean commentator and observer, but in addition as philosopher and judge. He is the only person capable of matching and outwitting Mrs Cheveley, since he has intimate knowledge of her stemming from their past encounter and, indeed, engagement; even now she wishes to marry him to cement her social and economic position. It is clear from his part in the play's scheme that he is morally, intellectually and aesthetically superior to everyone else. As Wilde describes him, 'One sees that he stands in immediate relation to modern life, makes it indeed, and so masters it. He is the first well-dressed philosopher in the history of thought.' Apart from his ability to manipulate events, his superiority is expressed by his decision to distance himself from the world of affairs. He placates his crustily benign father Lord Caversham by marrying the witty Mabel Chiltern; but his own career, as he prefers, is to be entirely domestic. At the close of Act Four the prospective 'ideal husband' goes out with his father and the woman who wants only to be 'oh! a real wife to him'. The closing stage image of the main-plot hero and heroine is subtly diminished by this exit.

The playfulness which surrounds Lord Goring is one of Wilde's most assured achievements. In *Lady Windermere's Fan* he had difficulty in reconciling the witty Lord Darlington with the serious lover; in *A Woman of No Importance* he struggled with the problem of the callous dandy; here he contrives to distance Lord Goring by matching him with an apparently frivolous, witty and unsentimental heroine. From time to time, indeed, the play comes to a virtual standstill while usually Lord Goring, less often some other of the 'trivial' characters, are allowed to play purely with words. Mrs Marchmont and Lady Basildon, Mabel Chiltern and Lord Caversham, provide a vein of light wit which encapsulates the unserious love-match, the counterpoint to the Chiltern's earnest marriage:

MABEL CHILTERN: You are always telling me your bad qualities, Lord
Goring.
LORD GORING: I have only told you half of them as yet, Miss Mabel!
MABEL CHILTERN: Are the others very bad?
LORD GORING: Quite dreadful! When I think of them at night I go to
sleep at once.
MABEL CHILTERN: Well, I delight in your bad qualities. I wouldn't have
you part with one of them.[37]

This shared mask of frivolity, a preliminary sketch for Cecily and
Algernon, serves as a refreshing contrast to the solemnity of Lady
Chiltern's attitude to life. It recurs later in the same act when Lord
Goring takes charge of the diamond brooch:

LORD GORING: I am going to make a rather strange request of you, Miss
Mabel.
MABEL CHILTERN [eagerly]: Oh, pray do! I have been waiting for it all
the evening.[37]

This is Wilde inclining towards a new kind of comedy in his knowing manipulation of dramatic convention. Another passage where
Wilde seems on the point of modulating into a different genre is
at the opening of Act Four:

LORD GORING [pulls out his watch, inspects it, and rings the bell]: It is a great
nuisance. I can't find anyone in this house to talk to. And I
am full of interesting information. I feel like the latest edition
of something or other.[38]

Lord Goring, one feels, needs to be in another play to find someone suitable to talk to (apart from himself, or his author, to whom
he bears a striking resemblance). But the classic location is the
opening exchange between him and the Ideal Butler, Phipps, who
'represents the dominance of form':

LORD GORING: For the future a more trivial buttonhole, Phipps, on
Thursday evenings.
PHIPPS: I will speak to the florist, my lord. She has had a loss in her
family lately, which perhaps accounts for the lack of triviality
your lordship complains of in the buttonhole.
LORD GORING: Extraordinary thing about the lower classes in England
– they are always losing their relations.
PHIPPS: Yes, my lord. They are extremely fortunate in that respect.[39]

This conversation begins to establish a comic style and ambiance
which Wilde eventually contrives to subordinate to the world of
international finance and the Foreign Office, but only with a sense

99

of loss. The play, as a well-constructed vehicle, functions adequately. The mechanical elements, the pair of letters, even the diamond brooch which Lord Goring transforms into a manacling bracelet, need not obtrude unduly, especially if they are handled as delicately as Wilde doubtless intended. Only the too-convenient falling of the chair in Act Three, as Shaw noted, betrays Wilde in an uncharacteristic carelessness. Yet it is the sub-plot, and the sub-text, with its increasingly insistent emphasis on form and style, which give the play its chief distinction and delight.

The contemporary, political glances are not nearly so far-fetched as some reviewers suggested, especially if they are approached as representative, even metaphoric, rather than as narrowly realistic. The use which David Hare and Howard Brenton make of political structures and events in *Pravda* is not dissimilar; and once again, the plays of Ibsen come to mind, for example *The Pillars of Society*. There is a greater assurance and sharpness in *An Ideal Husband*, generated in part no doubt by Wilde's growing confidence, in part by a sense of new developments in English contemporary drama. Pinero's *The Second Mrs Tanqueray* had appeared in June 1893, while Wilde had admired Shaw's *Widower's Houses* and his 'superb confidence in the dramatic value of the mere facts of life'.[40] It may have been partly a self-protective gesture which led Shaw to emphasise the 'subtle and pervading levity' of *An Ideal Husband*, and to protest that it was 'useless to describe a play which has no thesis: which is, in the purest integrity, a play and nothing less'.[41] When Wilde proceeded to create a 'pure' play, with *The Importance of Being Earnest*, Shaw complained that it had no heart. *An Ideal Husband* contrives to remain, like its ending, lightly equivocal, suggesting a thesis but refusing to state it.

7

Plays: *Salomé*

Wilde was writing *Salomé* during the closing months of 1891, when he was in Paris. Wilfrid Blunt's diary for 27 October records a breakfast with Wilde, 'on which occasion Oscar told us he was writing a play in French to be acted in the Français'.[1] The impulse to write in French, anticipating Beckett, may be understood in a number of ways. Wilde undoubtedly felt himself closer to the French in temperament than to the English, though he tended to exaggerate the warmth and admiration that the French expressed for him and his work. The high status of the artist in France, imbibed in his own case from the French-influenced Whistler, matched his own concept. Apart from these instinctive promptings, Wilde's later explanation suggests a recognition of the specific quality of the language of *Salomé*: 'I have one instrument I know that I can command, and that is the English language. There was another instrument to which I had listened all my life, and I wanted once to touch this new instrument to see whether I could make any beautiful thing out of it.'[2] Wilde often referred to *Salomé* in musical terms. In *De Profundis*, instancing the notes of doom in his works, he described it as 'one of the refrains whose recurring *motifs* make *Salomé* so like a piece of music and bind it together as a ballad';[3] and, in a later letter, 'The recurring phrases of *Salomé*, that bind it together like a piece of music with recurring *motifs*, are, and were to me, the artistic equivalent of the refrains of old ballads.'[4] Although Wilde spoke French fluently enough, he not unnaturally used the instrument of the French language in an idiosyncratic way; he also submitted a draft to a number of French friends for correction. The orthodoxy of his French is perhaps only marginally relevant, in the context of so original a work as *Salomé*; though Philippe Jullian offers an interesting French perspective: 'Oscar wrote a flowery French in which the anglicisms were acceptable as they gave a real ingenuousness to the babbling of Salomé and a strange majesty to Herod's speeches. In order that certain words should stand out as the author intended, *Salomé* has to be acted with an English accent.'⁵ The use of a second language allowed Wilde to stand at a certain distance from his material, giving *Salomé*, in both the French and English versions, an unusual verbal texture.

The process of the play's translation into English is somewhat obscure. *Salomé* was published in French in February 1893, in both Paris and London. The English translation followed almost a year later. Although this was dedicated 'To my friend Lord Alfred Bruce Douglas, the translator of my play', Wilde expressed deep dissatisfaction with Douglas's attempt, even proposing that Beardsley should undertake another version. In *De Profundis*, Wilde cites the translation as the catalyst for quarrels with Douglas. 'Three months later still, in September, new scenes occurred, the occasion of them being my pointing out the schoolboy faults of your attempted translation of *Salomé*. You must by this time be a fair enough French scholar to know that the translation was as unworthy of you, as an ordinary Oxonian, as it was of the work it sought to render.'⁶ It is reasonable to suppose that Wilde revised Douglas's draft to the point where it became his own once more. Had one no knowledge of Douglas's involvement, there would be little hesitation in assuming Wilde's total control.

In his choice of subject, Wilde associated himself with French romantic literature in general and, specifically, with the French symbolists. There is a great number of referents and sources, and it is useful to be aware of the more striking if only to emphasise the centrality of *Salomé*, whose interrupted and postponed theatrical history, no less than the unusual nature of the work, makes it harder to assess than Wilde's other plays.

Huysmans's *A Rebours*, which had 'partly suggested' the poison book in *The Picture of Dorian Gray*, contains in Chapter 5 an extended passage which describes Des Esseintes's pictures. 'He had bought Moreau's two masterpieces, and night after night he would stand dreaming in front of one of them, the picture of Salome.'⁷ While almost every line of the chapter could be argued to hold some relevance, there are three features in particular which bear upon Wilde's work. The first is the inherently dramatic potential within the description of each picture. The moments which each depicts – Salomé's dance, and her reaction to the Saint's severed head – are necessarily fixed; Huysmans's description of them is conceived in terms of movement, a response accentuated by the contrasting 'immobile statuesque' figure of Herod:

incense was burning, sending up clouds of vapour through which the fiery
gems set in the sides of the throne gleamed like the phosphorescent eyes
of wild animals. The clouds rose higher and higher, swirling under the
arches of the roof . . . Salome slowly glides forward on the points of her
toes . . . she begins the lascivious dance which is to rouse the aged Herod's
dormant senses; her breasts rise and fall, the nipples hardening at the
touch of her whirling necklaces; the strings of diamonds glitter against her
moist flesh; her bracelets, her belts, her rings all spit out fiery sparks;[8]

In addition, by his juxtaposition of the two moments (the dance,
and Salomé with the head), Huysmans explores the potent dramatic progression within the story.

Secondly, although Huysmans emphasises the erotic element in
each picture, in the actual description both of Salomé and of her
effect on the observer (Herod and Des Esseintes), he also indicates
the spiritual qualities or, more precisely, the tension between the
physical and spiritual in the concept of Salomé, evoking a dream-
like, superhuman figure:

Here she was no longer just the dancing-girl who extorts a cry of lust and
lechery from an old man by the lascivious movements of her loins; who
saps the morale and breaks the will of a king with the heaving of her
breasts, the twitching of her belly, the quivering of her thighs. She had
become, as it were, the symbolic incarnation of undying Lust, the Goddess of immortal Hysteria, the accursed Beauty exalted above all other
beauties by the catalepsy that hardens her flesh and steels her muscles, the
monstrous Beast, indifferent, irresponsible, insensible, poisoning, like the
Helen of ancient myth, everything that approaches her, everything that
sees her, everything that she touches.[9]

Wilde's Salomé is throughout less erotic, more virginal than
Huysmans's; yet his extended exploration of the Body/Soul,
Flesh/Spirit opposition seems a development of indications in *A
Rebours*, for example the phrases relating to the descriptions of the
dance, 'With a withdrawn, solemn, almost august expression on
her face', or 'her eyes fixed in the concentrated gaze of a
sleepwalker'.

Thirdly, and here the example of Huysmans is less specific, the
passage contains a forceful aesthetic apologia in its praise for an
artist who has crossed the 'frontiers' of his own sphere, to the
extent that Des Esseintes was 'disconcerted by this art which
crossed the frontiers of painting to borrow from the writer's art its
most subtly evocative suggestions, from the enameller's art its
most wonderfully brilliant effects, from the lapidary's and etcher's
art its most exquisitely delicate touches'. In his heavily charged

and supple prose, Huysmans provides an analogy for the quasi-musical mode in which Wilde conceived his *Salomé*. He provides, too, an analogy for Wilde's use of the whole range of arts embraced by his modernist concept of theatre. Wilde's claim in a letter to Douglas is entirely in tune with the idea from *A Rebours* quoted above:

> If I were asked of myself as a dramatist, I would say that my unique position was that I had taken the Drama, the most objective form known to art, and made it as personal a mode of expression as the Lyric or the Sonnet, while enriching the characterisation of the stage, and enlarging – at any rate in the case of *Salomé* – its artistic horizon.[10]

Huysmans's handling of the Salomé symbol is everywhere suggestive of Wilde's approach. There were several other recent treatments of Salomé which may at the least have promoted Wilde's interest in the subject: Laforgue's Salomé in *Moralités Légendaires*; Mallarmé's *Hérodiade*, with its musico-dramatic structure of *Ouverture*, *Scène* and the *Cantique de Saint Jean*; Flaubert's *Hérodias*. The overall tone of the Flaubert has particular affinities with Wilde's, and there are many verbal echoes. It is, perhaps, in Flaubert's description of the dance, which he holds back until the close of the story, that one may recognise the semi-mystical quality which Wilde developed in his own concept of Salomé: Flaubert's Salomé danced 'comme une Psyché curieuse, comme une âme vagabonde . . . Elle dansa comme les prêtresses des Indes, comme les Nubiennes des cataractes, comme les bacchantes de Lydie.'[11] In Mallarmé, it is the self-absorbed, cold purity of Hérodiade's vision which prefigures Wilde's Salomé:

> Le blond torrent de mes cheveux immaculés
> Quand il baigne mon corps solitaire le glace
> D'horreur, et mes cheveux que la lumière enlace
> Sont immortels. Ô femme, un baiser me tûrait
> Si la beauté n'était la mort . . .

(The blonde flood of my spotless hair, when it bathes my solitary body, ices it with horror, and my hair entwined with the light is immortal. O woman, a kiss would kill me, if beauty were not death . . .[12]

In terms of dramatic influences on *Salomé*, there are two aspects which particularly require comment. The first is the work of Maeterlinck. Wilde cited the Flemish Maeterlinck as an example of a playwright who achieved a special effect by writing in an 'alien' language; he also acknowledged him, together with Hugo, as the only modern playwrights who had interested him. Katharine Worth has emphasised the influence on Wilde of

Maeterlinck's *La Princesse Maleine*, published in 1889, for the English translation of which Wilde was invited to write an introduction; 'In both plays a very young heroine is overwhelmed by a passion which drives her inexorably to a violent death.'[13] More specifically, Maeterlinck makes extensive use of the repetition of simple phrases, which lends a dream-like quality to the verbal texture; he also employs scenic elements in a way similar to Wilde. Indeed, the beginning of *La Princesse Maleine*, with its choric commentary from detached observers, provides a model that is reflected in Wilde's own opening scene, and which serves to clarify the consciousness of both writers of the Shakespearean archetypes. Maeterlinck's first scene is set in the castle gardens. Two officers comment on the signs in the sky – the moon, the clouds, comet, stars – and on the celebrations within:

On dit que ses étoiles à longue chevelure annoncent la mort des princesses.[14]

Herodias's page similarly associates the signs in the heavens with the death of a woman:

Regardez la lune. La lune a l'air très étrange. On dirait une femme qui sort d'un tombeau. Elle ressemble à une femme morte. On dirait qu'elle cherche des morts.[15]

If Wilde clearly echoes and develops something of Maeterlinck's verbal music, it is in scenic terms that *La Princesse Maleine* is most suggestive. Within the brief space of the opening scene Maeterlinck's directions include: 'Ici une comète apparaît au-dessus du château'; 'Ici une pluie d'étoiles semble tomber sur le château'; 'Ici les fenêtres du château, illuminées au fond du jardin, volent en éclats: cris, rumeurs, tumulte.' First, the Princess leaves the betrothal feast and, finally, the drunken King Hjalmar erupts with his officers and retinue into the garden. If one adds the lighting indication, 'Le ciel devient noir, et la lune est étrangement rouge', there are ample indications of both structure and symbol within the one scene alone for Wilde to develop. More generally, Maeterlinck's insistent use of colour, sound, dance, visual description and visual effect offered Wilde a theatrical vocabulary more complete and more innovative than anything the London stage could demonstrate.

Wilde's earlier romantic dramas, *Vera* and *The Duchess of Padua*, contain some previous explorations of the ideas of *Salomé*; they also demonstrated techniques to avoid. *The Duchess of Padua*, though written some nine years before, had finally achieved production in New York in 1891; and for a time Wilde attempted to promote a London production, inviting Irving to reconsider the text. Although *The Duchess of Padua* is full of interesting and imaginative theatrical concepts, it is so diffuse and so palpably derivative that it can only have stimulated Wilde in his instinct to create a more individual and truly modern method and style. Wilde's belated admission, '*The Duchess* is unfit for publication – the only one of my works that comes under that category',[16] is a recognition of the unsuitability of his use of blank verse as a dramatic medium. However, the central idea in *The Duchess of Padua*, the impulse towards a particularly intense mode of romantic, individualistic self-fulfilment, is taken up by Wilde in *Salomé*. Wilde's letter to Mary Anderson, the American actress whom he hoped would accept the former play and the role, isolates the heart of the drama in Act Three:

Here there is no need of comedy: the act is short, quick, terrible: what we want is to impress the audience clearly with the two great speculations and problems of the play, the relations of Sin and Love: they must see that both Guido and the Duchess have rights on their side: Guido is cruel, and the Duchess has done wrong: but they represent great principles of Life and Love.[17]

Wilde was at this point locked into concepts of character that he would later feel free to abandon, just as he would abandon the different modes of comedy which he consciously adopted here in response to his theory that an audience will not weep if you have not made them laugh.

Salomé has an intensity, a rapidity of effect, that is in marked contrast to Wilde's previous poetic drama, or, indeed, to *La Princesse Maleine*. The play is organised through a prelude, or introduction, followed by three major episodes: the first encounter between Salomé and Jokanaan, in the phase of the white moon, marked by the death of the young Syrian; the central episode, the phase of the red moon, which moves towards the crucial actions of the dance of the seven veils and the beheading of Jokanaan; and the swift and terrible conclusion, when the black cloud conceals the moon, and Salomé is crushed to death beneath the soldiers' shields. The tripartite pattern indicated by the three deaths and the three colours of the moon forms the prevailing rhythm of the play; but because Wilde handles it skilfully it never becomes automatic or predictable. The inevitability is only apparent once the pattern is complete, and the three parts are so concentrated and interlocking that it is the work's unity which is its most remarkable characteristic.

The mode of repetition is established during the introduction, set on the terrace of Herod's palace, between the unseen banqueting hall, where Herod is feasting the ambassadors of Caesar, and the bronze cistern where Jokanaan is imprisoned. The stage disposition suggests the separation of the material and the spiritual, with the terrace serving as the meeting-place, the arena of conflict. Wilde widens this scheme of reference by his use of the soldiers to indicate both the universality of the Roman Empire geographically, and the multiplicity of spiritual traditions which it embraced. For examples, there are the speeches of the Nubian: 'The gods of my country are very fond of blood'; the Cappadocian: 'In my country there are no gods left'; and the first Soldier: 'The Jews worship a God you cannot see.'[18] Similarly, while the soldiers introduce the key motif of Herod's obsession with Salomé:

FIRST SOLDIER: He is looking at something.
SECOND SOLDIER: He is looking at someone.

Wilde has already laid out a more complex and resonant pattern through the Young Syrian's repeated:

How beautiful is the Princess Salomé tonight.

and the ominous commentary of the Page of Herodias, himself in love with the unnoticing Syrian:

You are always looking at her. You look at her too much. It is dangerous to look at people in such fashion. Something terrible may happen.

These opening speeches are remarkable in their powers of suggestion. Wilde succeeds in introducing many of the central ideas, symbols and motifs with lucid precision: the beauty of the Princess Salomé; the ominous association between her and the moon; the death-wish; the idea of the dance; the obsession of Herod with Salomé. These motifs are merely placed, like the first statements of musical phrases. But the dramatic method has also been established. The key word lies in the play's first action: the act of looking, as the Young Syrian looks at Salomé, followed by Herod 'looking at someone', and by Salomé looking at Jokanaan. The word is taken up by speaker after speaker. It is contrasted in this opening phase with what is heard: first the uproar of the Jews disputing in the banqueting hall, and secondly the prophetic utterance of Jokanaan (whom Herod has forbidden to be seen) promising the coming of the Son of Man. Wilde moves the play towards the encounter between two idealised and contrasting figures, Salomé the perfection of beauty and Jokanaan the inspired prophet.

It is important to be alert to the way in which Wilde presents Salomé in this early phase of the play. We have first been given a series of isolated definitions: 'She is like a princess who has little white doves for feet', at once followed by the Page's comment about the moon, which becomes transferred to Salomé: 'She is like a woman who is dead.' The tension between the two statements of innocence and experience is expressed by Salomé herself in her self-defining opening speech:

Why does the Tetrarch look at me all the while with his mole's eyes under his shaking eyelids? It is strange that the husband of my mother looks at me like that. I know not what it means. In truth, yes, I know it.[19]

It is also revealed in her own response to the moon, which she compares, as she herself has just been compared, to 'a little silver flower' but first, within the same sentence, to 'a little piece of money'. The moon must be a virgin; but her virginity is defined by negatives: 'She has never defiled herself'; 'She has never abandoned herself to men, like the other goddesses.'

Against this vision of self-delighting, cold virginity Wilde places Jokanaan's announcement, 'The Lord hath come. The Son of Man hath come.' Wilde's Jokanaan is a more elusive creation even than Salomé, since he comes with a weightier apparatus of historical and theological reference. In addition to the literary antecedents, Wilde has used both biblical and historical sources with considerable freedom. Just as Wilde's Herod incorporates elements of Herod Antipas and Herod Agrippa in addition to Herod the Tetrarch, so his Jokanaan at times seems identified with the John familiar from the synoptic Gospels, but at others serves as a vehicle for a much less specific prophetic tradition. This enables Wilde to construct his own apocryphal text, with quotation, semi-quotation and echo ranging from Isaiah to the Book of Revelation. Jokanaan, like Salomé, has multiple functions. He is the mouthpiece of Christianity, which opposes the romantic paganism of Salomé. He presents an image of ascetic spirituality, and in the intense pursuit of this ideal attracts the attention of both Salomé and Herod. In symbolic terms, he is the outcast, the scapegoat, the criminal, the subversive, isolated by the state because of the threat he poses to its stability. In the context of the play's wider concerns, he is the voice of the Apocalypse, ushering in the last days of the world.

His sharpest delineation occurs in his reaction to Salomé, and in hers to him. Initially, it is his utterance which arouses her: 'Of whom is he speaking?'; 'But he is terrible, he is terrible!'; 'Do you think he will speak again?'; 'Speak again, Jokanaan. Thy voice is wine to me.' The series of comments becomes crystallised into a personal request: 'Speak again! Speak again, Jokanaan, and tell me what I must do.'[20]

Salomé's plea is rejected – rejection, isolation, is the characteristic state of the world of the play – in Jokanaan's pivotal speech:

Daughter of Sodom, come not near me! but cover thy face with a veil, and scatter ashes upon thy head, and get thee to the desert and seek out the Son of Man.

Salomé's question, 'Who is he, the Son of Man? Is he as beautiful as thou art, Jokanaan?', is answered by Jokanaan in a phrase deliberately reminiscent of Christ's temptation in the wilderness: 'Get thee behind me! I hear in the palace the beatings of the wings of the angel of death.' By the pattern of association already established, the image of the angel of death is inevitably linked with Salomé herself; while the submerged reference to the Satanic, following upon Salomé's speech ascribing beauty to the Son of Man, emphasises the dichotomy of spiritual and physical, and of good and evil. The play proceeds to what is both a symbolic re-enactment of the Fall, and a highly charged, ritualistic attempt at synthesis, as Salomé assumes a prophetic role in her own search for fulfilment.

The address to Jokanaan moves through three stages. First, Salomé declares her love of Jokanaan's white body: 'Thy body is white like the lilies of a field that the mower hath never mowed . . . Let me touch thy body.' When Jokanaan repels her – 'By woman came evil into the world' – Salomé's veneration turns to disgust: 'Thy body is hideous. It is like the body of a leper', and her attention shifts to his black hair: 'There is nothing in the world so black as thy hair . . . Let me touch thy hair.' Rejected once more by Jokanaan, the hair becomes horrible, 'like a crown of thorns which they have placed on thy forehead', and Salomé desires instead Jokanaan's red mouth. As she repeats, as though in a trance, 'I will kiss thy mouth, Jokanaan', the Young Syrian

109

kills himself and falls between the two opposed figures. Three times Salomé is told of the death, by the Page of Herodias, by the Soldier, and by Jokanaan. Salomé only repeats, this time as a plea, 'Let me kiss thy mouth', followed by a return to the more ominous prophetic mode, 'I will kiss thy mouth.'[21] Jokanaan descends into the cistern, into the place of darkness made more terrible by the events that have occurred in the moonlight, while Salomé remains silent, isolated, absorbed in the singleness of her vision.

After the brief elegy for the Young Syrian, the play moves abrasively into its central, public sequence with the entrance of Herod, Herodias and all the court. The sequence begins with disturbing echoes of the play's opening. The First Soldier's statement, 'The Tetrarch will not come to this place. He never comes on the terrace. He is too much afraid of the prophet', is immediately contradicted by Herod's arrival: it has already been established that when what should not happen occurs – the Young Syrian looking at Salomé, the appearance of Jokanaan from the cistern – something terrible ensues. The essential unity of the action is further cemented by verbal parallels: Herodias's 'You must not look at her' repeats the Page's earlier warnings, while Herod's next speech, on the moon, reinforces the association. However, the development of Herod's ideas shifts the poetic key into something much more jagged and raw: 'She is like a mad woman, a mad woman who is seeking everywhere for lovers. She is naked, too . . . She reels through the clouds like a drunken woman . . .' Herod's words indicate the affinity of his imagination with that of Salomé; while the blood on which he slips, and his perception of the wind – 'something that is like the beating of wings' – links him with Jokanaan. In contrast is the deliberate literalism of Herodias: 'the moon is like the moon, that is all'; 'there is a wind'.

Wilde's dramatic treatment of the episode whose climax is the dance is unusual in its obliqueness. There are four principal elements, centred upon and seen in relation to the persona of Herod: Salomé, Jokanaan, the court (Romans, Jews, Nazarenes), and Herodias. Salomé is defined first by her three denials of Herod: 'I am not thirsty, Tetrarch', 'I am not hungry, Tetrarch', 'I am not tired, Tetrarch'; [22] she remains silent thereafter, in reverie, until she is invited to dance. The voice of Jokanaan invades the terrace, initiating the successive definitions of God, but also increasingly insulting to Herodias. The dramatic method serves to accentuate the distinctiveness of each of the four main characters, while simultaneously increasing the tension between them. Herod, the symbol of earthly power, is associated with the spirituality of Jokanaan which opposes him; the epithets Jokanaan hurls at Herodias – 'Ah, the daughter of Babylon with her golden eyes and her gilded eyelids' – already spoken in her daughter's presence, inevitably draw our attention also to the contrasting shadow-image of Salomé.

The speech which signals the shift from prelude to action is, appropriately, Jokanaan's apocalyptic prophecy. Wilde gives him a scarcely altered, though condensed, speech based on the passage from the Book of Revelation which records what was written beneath the sixth seal:

In that day the sun shall become black like sackcloth of hair, and the moon shall become like blood, and the stars of the heavens shall fall upon the earth like ripe figs that fall from the fig tree, and the kings of the earth shall be afraid.[23]

The springboard for Jokanaan's prophecy is Herod's reference to Salomé's pallor, and Herodias's reiterated warning, 'You must not look at her', so that Salomé herself becomes a sign of the apocalypse. Jokanaan's speech also initiates the play's next phase, that of the blood-red moon. Significantly, Herodias responds positively to the content of his words: ' I should like to see that day of which he speaks . . .' Herod's explanation, 'It may be he is drunk with the wine of God', with its symbiotic recognition of Jokanaan's imaginative state, forms the context for his ensuing preoccupation, represented by the stage-direction: 'from this point he looks all the while at Salomé'. The public complexities of the court have become simplified into an intense concentration upon the four principal figures, and upon the transformational action of the anticipated dance, the dramatic form which responds to the apocalyptic mode of the language.

In the dialogue which prefaces the dance itself, Wilde accentuates by means of repitition a cluster of motifs and images. The sexual dimension of the dance is stressed through Herod's three invitations to Salomé to dance, all of which are denied, to the delight of Herodias; but these are complicated by the references to incest contained within Jokanaan's condemnation of Herod's marriage with Herodias, and the counter accusations of sterility. The idea of the dance, already carrying symbolic weight, is further overlaid with intimations of death, first through Jokanaan's

111

prophecy, 'He shall be eaten of worms', and secondly through Herod who reintroduces the motifs of slipping in blood and of the beating of wings. When Salomé indicates her willingness to dance, a change signalled by her rising to her feet, the pressure upon the dance itself is further intensified, by Herodias's attempts to dissuade her, and by Herod's confused anticipatory responses. His sense of the nearness of death is expressed through packed references to beatings of wings, a huge black bird, a wind that is first icy, then hot, and to the garland of roses on his forehead that burns him, with petals like stains of blood – a surprising, but momentary, extension of Herod into a Christ figure, assisted by references to crucifixion.

During the physical preparations for the dance ('Slaves bring perfumes and the seven veils, and take off the sandals of Salomé'),[24] the paradoxical associations of Salomé are clarified. Herod says to her, 'Your little feet will be like white doves', recalling the Young Syrian's praise; but this idea of virginal innocence is at once countered by the recollection of the blood already spilt on the ground. It is at this point, too, that Herod notices that the moon 'has become red as blood', in fulfilment of Jokanaan's prophecy, while Jokanaan's voice is heard for the last time, in a quotation from Isaiah's vision of the Son of Man: 'Who is this who cometh from Edom . . . whose raiment is dyed with purple?'

The most enigmatic aspect of *Salomé* is the laconic stage-direction, 'Salomé dances the dance of the seven veils'. Since Wilde was prevented from overseeing a production, it is impossible to be certain how he would have wished it to be executed: the question is discussed later in this chapter. Attention to the preceding dialogue, and to the images and motifs, can only indicate the weight and dramatic significance which the dance must carry: after the complexities and paradoxes of language, the silent, expressive and progressive statement of movement. One may at least assume that the merely erotic is both inadequate and inappropriate.

The sequence which follows the dance centres upon Salomé's request to Herod. In a striking departure from the Gospel narrative, Salomé does not ask for Herodias's advice. Rather she expresses her wish directly, so linking the request to her earlier prophecy to Jokanaan, 'I will kiss thy mouth.' She asks eight times in all, with intermittent support from Herodias. In response, Herod makes four major attempts to divert her. Three of these propose substitutes: the emerald, the white peacocks, and lastly a

long list of treasure which concludes with the most valuable and
dangerous gift Herod can conceive of, the veil of the sanctuary.
The speech which precedes this offer, the third of the series,
expresses Herod's perception of Jokanaan's holiness, 'The finger
of God has touched him', and his fear that his own death is involved with the fate of Jokanaan: 'Salomé, you do not wish a
misfortune to happen to me?' Wilde, in fact, is careful to explore
the extent to which Herod's self-knowledge and self-judgment is
bound up in Salomé's request: 'It may be that I have loved you
too much'; 'Your beauty has grievously troubled me, and I have
looked at you too much. But I will look at you no more.'[25]

The play has reached its climactic, intensified phase, where
Wilde deploys stage movement and visual image with power and
precision, in conjunction with Salomé's final long speech. Once
again, just as with the dance, Wilde prepares the climactic
moments with great skill: the ring of death is taken from Herod's
hand by Herodias, and conveyed to the Executioner; the Executioner descends into the cistern; Salomé, waiting for the death cry,
demands that others be sent down to carry out the execution.
Then comes the terrible image: 'A huge black arm, the arm of the
Executioner, comes forth from the cistern, bearing on a silver
shield the head of Jokanaan.'[26] Salomé's speech, delivered to the
severed head while Herod hides his face with his cloak, constitutes
the most disturbing and ambivalent passage of the play. It is
delivered within a context of the stated, impending action, that
Salomé will kiss Jokanaan's dead mouth. Yet that action is
acknowledged to be essentially negative, self-destructive,
catastrophic. Even Salomé, in her state of ecstasy, recognises that
Jokanaan cannot look at her: 'Thine eyes that were so terrible, so
full of rage and scorn, are shut now'; 'Well, thou hast seen thy
God, Jokanaan, but me, me, thou didst never see.' Her love for
Jokanaan is stated and developed in the past tense, before its
tragic restatement in the present. 'Oh, how I loved thee! I love thee
yet, Jokanaan, I love thee only . . .' At the very end of the speech
Wilde's control falters, with a conclusion uneasily reminiscent of
the forced wisdom of the prose poems and stories: 'Well I know
that thou wouldst have loved me, and the mystery of love is greater
than the mystery of death. Love only should one consider.' This
seems both too weakly phrased and too simplistic to serve in itself
as the immediate cue for Herod's violent reaction. It may be that
the lines were intended as the accompaniment of action, however,
as Salomé approaches, or handles, the severed head.

The play's last moments form a highly charged and compressed sequence of dramatic images. Herod is appalled at Salomé's actions, Herodias approving. Herod orders the torches to be put out, for 'I will not look at things. I will not suffer things to look at me.' He refers not only to the evidence of the crime that has been done, but to the terrible action to which Salomé is committed. Wilde now darkens the stage, for the final phase of the moon: 'The slaves put out the torches. The stars disappear. A great black cloud crosses the moon and conceals it completely. The stage becomes very dark. The Tetrarch begins to climb the staircase.' Out of the darkness comes Salomé's voice, announcing, 'I have kissed thy mouth, Jokanaan.' A moonbeam falls on her, covering her with light, and Herod's last order, 'Kill that woman!' is carried out, as the guards crush Salomé to death beneath their shields.

The sequence provides an active, terse, direct resolution to a play which has been reflective, expansive and circuitous in exposition. It crystallises through the actions and words of the central characters the lyrical images with which the play began, placed then through the peripheral figures of the Young Syrian and the Page of Herodias: 'How beautiful is the Princess Salomé tonight!'; 'Look at the moon! How strange the moon seems! She is like a woman rising from a tomb. She is like a dead woman. You would fancy she was looking for dead things.' Herod's order to kill is, appropriately, a response to the fatal act of looking which was stated and developed in the opening scene. The play, so concentrated in its focus upon the charismatic figures of Jokanaan and Salomé, gains an additional and unexpected dimension through the transference of interest to the person of Herod, whose perceptions and reactions emerge to form an ironic, detached commentary upon the action.

That the play's last moments emphasise the perceiver, the gazer, in relation to the image that is contemplated indicates one way to approach the work as a whole. This approach is easier to pay lip-service to than to put into practice, especially in the absence of an early production under Wilde's influence and with the later and misleading overlay of Strauss's *Salome* as an inevitable distraction. The importance of the perceiver is a reminder of some of Wilde's play's analogues, for example Heine's poem *Atta Troll*. On the eve of St John's day, under the full moon, the poet observes a wild procession which goes past him three times; among the figures is Herodias, carrying the charger with John's head in it, which she kisses and tosses in the air like a ball, catching it again and laughing like a child. Long after the poet still sees the procession in his mind's eye, and wonders why Herodias nodded and looked at him so lovingly.

The space which the intervention of the poet, the perceiver, places between the reader and the image has to be achieved in *Salomé* through a particular style of performance. In *Romantic Image*, Frank Kermode traces the image of the dancer, and in particular its manifestations through various Salomes, in Yeats's work: 'Salome is the Dancer in the special role of the Image that costs the artist personal happiness, indeed life itself.' He goes on in a paragraph which is illuminating for Wilde's Salomé:

When Richard Strauss heard Elisabeth Schumann sing, he expressed a great desire to hear her in the role of Salome; and when she protested the apparently obvious unsuitability of her voice, he explained that what the part needed was not some heroic soprano (which is in fact what we usually get) but precisely the transparent, even girlish, clarity of her tone. Unhappily nothing came of the proposal, but it seems clear that Strauss was not talking eccentrically, and that he had recognized in Mme Schumann's voice the possibility of her achieving some vocal equivalent for that unemotional, disengaged quality – Yeats's word might be 'uncommitted' – which Wilde gave his Salome, and which, despite the ridicule of critics, was fundamental to his conception of her. There should be an innocent, totally destructive malice; beauty inhumanly immature and careless cruelty. This is the type.[27]

The centrality of the dance, and the disengaged detachment of the dancer, were explored by Yeats, particularly in the dance-plays founded on the theatrical form and techniques of the Japanese Noh. In *At the Hawk's Well*, the Woman of the Sidhe's dance constitutes the central episode; and by looking on her Cuchulain becomes doomed to the life of a tragic hero. The same Woman dances in *The Only Jealousy of Emer*: the ghost of Cuchulain rises and follows her, crying out 'Your mouth! Your mouth!' In *A Full Moon in March*, the Queen gives orders for the singer, a candidate for her hand in marriage though presented to her in the foul form of a swineherd, to be beheaded, then dances before his severed head, a sequence developed in *The King of the Great Clock Tower*: here the singer's head is cut off, and the Queen dances with the head on her shoulder, before kissing it on the stroke of midnight. Finally, there is *The Death of Cuchulain*, and the Old Man's Prologue:

I wanted a dance, because where there are no words there is less to spoil.

115

Emer must dance, there must be severed heads – I am old, I belong to mythology – severed heads for her to dance before. I had thought to have had those heads carved, but no, if the dancer can dance properly no wood-carving can look as well as a parallelogram of painted wood. But I was at my wit's end to find a good dancer; I could have got such a dancer once, but she has gone; the tragi-comedian dancer, the tragic dancer, upon the same neck love and loathing, life and death.[28]

Yeats's Old Man spits three times upon 'the dancers painted by Degas', above all 'upon that chambermaid face. They might have looked timeless, Rameses the Great, but not the chambermaid, that old maid history.' Yeats's use of the dancer suggests a process of refining through successive experiments, until he reaches the purity of his last definition. It does not seem far from the kind of theatre Wilde was intuitively making.

The casting of Sarah Bernhardt as Salomé in itself indicated a non-realist approach. Graham Robertson, who was organising the costumes for the abortive London production, and who adopted a distinctly sceptical attitude towards the play, records asking Sarah Bernhardt, 'I suppose you will get a *figurante* to go through it, won't you? – veiled, of course, and with your blue hair?',[29] and being astonished to find that she intended to dance the Dance of the Seven Veils herself. However, the censor's banning of the play successfully masked the actress's intentions. Something of her approach may be deduced from a conversation reported by Charles Ricketts. When Wilde was reading *Salomé* to Sarah Bernhardt, 'She exclaimed "Mais, c'est héraldique, on dirait une fresque", and for days both author and actress discussed the pitch of voice required. "Le mot doit tomber comme une perle sur une disque de cristal, pas de mouvements rapides, des gestes stylisés." ' Ricketts adds, 'The music-hall tigress and blood lust of the Continental stage is of German invention.'[30] As Wilde wrote in his last months, 'What has age to do with acting? The only person in the world who could act Salomé is Sarah Bernhardt, that "serpent of old Nile", older than the pyramids.'[31]

Since style is the essence of *Salomé*, it is helpful to put together as much evidence as possible about Wilde's own production ideas. Graham Robertson claimed that he and Wilde had often talked over its possible production:

'I should like,' he said, throwing off the notion, I believe, at random, 'I should like everyone on the stage to be in yellow.'
It was a good idea and I saw its possibilities at once – every costume of some shade of yellow from clearest lemon to deep orange, with here and

there just a hint of black – yes, you must have that – and all upon a pale ivory terrace against a great empty sky of deepest violet.

'A violet sky,' repeated Oscar Wilde slowly. 'Yes – I never thought of that. Certainly a violet sky and then, in place of an orchestra, braziers of perfume. Think – the scented clouds rising and partly veiling the stage from time to time – a new perfume for each new emotion!'[32]

However, when Sarah Bernhardt agreed to include the play in her London season, there was no time for the braziers or even for the yellow scheme, and she made do with the costumes for *Cléopâtre*.

Another designer with whom Wilde discussed *Salomé*, and one infinitely more sympathetic to the nature of the work, was Charles Ricketts. Ricketts, as innovative a designer as Craig in some respects, was creatively involved in design concepts for *Salomé* for some twenty-five years. Wilde first approached him to design the production planned by Lugné-Poë for Paris (Lugné-Poë presented the play there when Wilde was in prison):

This first project did not materialise. I proposed a black floor, upon which Salomé's feet could move like white doves; this was said to capture the author. The sky was to be a rich turquoise green, cut by the perpendicular fall of gilded strips of Japanese matting forming an aerial tent above the terraces. Did Wilde suggest the division of the actors into separate masses of colour? To-day I cannot decide. The Jews were to be in yellow, John in white, and Herod and Herodias in blood-red. Over Salomé the discussions were endless; should she be clothed in black – like the night, in silver like the moon or – the suggestion was Wilde's – green like a curious poisonous lizard?[33]

Ricketts did designs for two productions of *Salomé*. The first was for the Literary Theatre Society, which presented *Salomé* in a double bill with *A Florentine Tragedy* at the King's Hall on 10 June 1906. This production encountered many constrictions, both of economy and of inexperience. Nevertheless, Ricketts's involvement ensured that something of Wilde's original approach remained. Ricketts

placed dim cypress-like curtains against a star-lit sky; the players were clothed in every shade of blue, deepening into dark violet and green, the general harmony of blue on blue being relieved by the red lances of the soldiers, and – shall I confess it? – owing to my nervousness in directing the limelight-man, the moon shone but very fitfully, generally after it had been mentioned in the text, and never once upon the floor![34]

Ricketts's diary entries form a revealing commentary on the progress of rehearsals: he appears gradually to have taken control of the direction – 'Dress rehearsal under my direction' – as well as the physical production. On the first night, he reported four curtain calls for *Salomé*, but also disappointment about Miss Darragh's dance, 'begun too soon, over too soon'.[35] The same reservation was expressed about the second performance on 18 June: 'The dance makes the difficulty, it ought to be a great point and here it is almost suppressed . . . '[36] Shaw and Duse were in the audience; the press, led by *The Times*, boycotted the production.

In 1919 Ricketts returned to the play, reconstructing *Salomé* for a proposed production by the Shochiku Theatrical Company of Tokyo. He recounted a dream version which gives a powerful idea of the style towards which he as designer was aiming. He dreamt

that Sada Yacco had performed *Salomé* in a Japanese version of the play; that, with strange muttered soliloquies she had descended a staircase haunted by her guilty passion for Herod; that John, a bound prisoner behind a wattle, had made ardent love to her till, in Japanese fashion, she had pushed the wattle back upon him with sudden birdlike cries interrupted by the terrific entrance of Kawakami as Herod with a convulsed mask, feet turned in, in a slow deliberate descent of the stairs, supported by a hesitating Herodias. I saw the dance, rapid, vivid, trance-like, the head thrust over the wattle, and Salome's suicide after a slow muttered speech spoken to space or to the audience she did not see.[37]

This dream-like vision was unrealisable: Ricketts added that the Japanese Salomé, whose photo he had seen, 'wears Maud Allan pearls in her hair'. The search for the image of the dance has continued, in such productions as Terence Gray's at the Festival Theatre, Cambridge in 1931, in which Beatrix Lehmann played Salomé with the dance choreographed by Ninette de Valois, or Lindsay Kemp's balletic version.

Ricketts's costume designs may never have reached Tokyo. But a synopsis he wrote for Robert Ross indicates the style and colour scheme:

Salomé, dressed in a mist rising by moonlight, with a train of blue and black moths. Herodias, in a peacock train of Dahlias and a horned tiara. Herod is robed in silver and blue lined with flame decorated with griffons, sphinxes and angels. The scene is all blue on blue.

Finally, there remains Ricketts's stage setting for *Salomé*, which is in the collection of the Fitzwilliam Museum, Cambridge. It seems to depict the opening sequence, with the figure of the Young Syrian gazing at the off-stage Salomé, and the Page of Herodias turned away towards the central group of soldiers, while the

Executioner stands in silhouette. The dominant colour is, indeed, blue: blue in the background and the hangings and drapes, turquoise on the floor. Ricketts breaks the blue with patches and flecks of other colours: the white circle of the cistern, the silver throne, blood-red on the pillars and on the soldiers' spears, flecks of gold on curtains, pillars and floor, green on the Young Syrian's costume. It makes a wholly appropriate setting for the costume concepts of the four major characters.

These notes and memories about the idea of the dance, and about the costumes and *décor*, provide some indications about the nature of Wilde's *Salomé*. It is a work which attracted vilification, and which almost invites ridicule. It demands a particular style of speech and movement, and an exquisite sensitivity of design. It is remarkable that Wilde, with scarcely any preliminary exploration, could create a truly modern symbolist drama within a theatrical and social context of such pronounced hostility.

8

Plays: *The Importance of Being Earnest*

The Importance of Being Earnest is widely regarded as Wilde's supreme achievement in drama, and by many as his most accomplished piece of work in any genre. The play's success and originality do not make it easier to discuss. The sub-title, 'A Trivial Comedy for Serious People', like Wilde's other definition, 'written by a butterfly for butterflies',[1] suggests the play's essential fragility. Auden called it 'the only pure verbal opera in English',[2] which indicates something of its special quality. Shaw, who did not 'greatly' care for the play, wrote that the 'general effect is that of a farcical comedy dating from the seventies, unplayed during that period because it was too clever and too decent, and brought up to date as far as possible by Mr Wilde in his now completely formed style'.[3] Twice Shaw invoked the name of Gilbert, as did many of the reviewers; and most placed it within the genre of farce. William Archer, whose criticism has one advantage over Shaw's, disinterestedness, pointed out that ' "farce" is far too gross and commonplace a word to apply to such an iridescent filament of fantasy'.[4] The essential difference, at least, between *The Importance of Being Earnest* and the preceding comedies is clear, and Wilde's last play has joined the narrow national repertory – indeed, the international repertory – without any of the qualifications attached to his other plays.

Wilde himself may not at first have realised how superior *The Importance of Being Earnest* was, though he was fully conscious of the differences in style. He sent his 'somewhat farcical comedy' to Alexander, under the cover title of *Lady Lancing*, commenting, perhaps to arouse Alexander's professional pride, that the play was 'not suitable to you at all: you are a romantic actor: the people it wants are actors like Wyndham and Hawtrey'.[5] The play, it seems, was passed on to Charles Wyndham, but when Henry James's historical drama *Guy Domville* failed at the St James's Theatre, Wyndham stepped aside to allow Alexander to mount a production early in 1895. The rehearsals followed swiftly on the opening of *An Ideal Husband*, which played at the Haymarket from 3 January.

Alexander's first contribution was to ask Wilde to reduce his four-act structure to three acts, ostensibly to allow time for a curtain-raiser. The four-act first draft has been published, and indeed performed occasionally. Its major difference is the intervention of the solicitor Gribsby, who follows Algernon to Hertfordshire with a writ for debts incurred at the Savoy Hotel, and ominously unfurls before him the prospect of Holloway Prison. There can be no doubt, however, that the three-act structure which Wilde produced for Alexander is infinitely more effective. The text was finally published in 1899, after it had been slightly but significantly expanded by Wilde, at a time when he desperately needed money, and when he was considering the play as a work to be read. The sparser acting text is dramatically superior. Wilde reportedly made such a nuisance of himself at rehearsals that Alexander encouraged him to go abroad: Wilde and Lord Alfred Douglas spent two weeks in North Africa at the end of January 1895.

The title, and its gloss, 'A Trivial Comedy for Serious People', invite comment. Shaw even suggested that Wilde was modelling himself on Henry Arthur Jones, by giving his play a 'five-chambered' title like *The Case of Rebellious Susan*. 'Trivial' and 'Serious' can clearly be taken in two ways: it was ironic that such a fellow-spirit as Shaw should be, for once, so conventional and Victorian in his seriousness. That Gwendolen and Cecily should have as an ideal someone of the name Ernest is ironic in a different way: the extent of the irony becomes increasingly apparent as their seriously expressed reasons are defined in all their triviality. The identification of Ernest-ness with the cant and hypocrisy of Victorian life is underlined by Samuel Butler's choice of the name Ernest Pontifex for his 'hero' in *The Way of All Flesh*, which was written though not published by this time, and which was rigorous in its condemnation of Victorian family life and its twin pillars of religion and education. Wilde's commentary, fully as decisive in effect, works in a much more oblique and subversive manner.

Wilde's major development in terms of dramatic structure is to solve the tension seen hitherto between the dandies and the Philistines, between form and content, between the trivial and the serious, by creating a sophisticated comic world that is entire and self-sufficient. We enter a kind of Arcadia or Illyria, and never leave it. There are no extraneous or threatening elements such as Gribsby and his writ might have posed, above all no Puritans. Jack Worthing and Algernon Moncrieff are as witty as Lord

OSCAR WILDE

Goring, but they are spared the strain of having to function as philosophers – or rather, their wit and manner constitute their philosophy. The seemingly innocent Gwendolen and Cecily are even more adroit than their lovers in standing every convention on its head and in manipulating each circumstance to their own advantage. Lady Bracknell from time to time looms darkly over the pattern; but the element of danger which she represents is simply a function of plot, when she enacts the traditional blocking role of the disapproving parent, and as the play proceeds it becomes evident that she herself has manipulated life for years. Besides, her idiosyncratic verbal exuberance elevates her to a different level of creation, and she develops in Act Three into a benevolent, if tyrannical, goddess like some comic distillation of the Red Queen and Queen Victoria. Canon Chasuble and Miss Prism, ostensibly the guardians of morality, are similarly made harmless by their distinctive and grotesque use of language, and are seduced from their priestly and pedagogic duties to the more pleasurable pursuit of each other.

Wilde achieved exceptional elegance and symmetry of form in *The Importance of Being Earnest*. The three-act structure proved an advantage, imposing an economy of setting and character. The play opens in London, in the morning-room of Algernon Moncrieff's flat; moves out to the old-fashioned garden, full of roses, at Jack Worthing's country house; and concludes in the country house drawing-room, looking out on to the garden. The action moves swiftly in time, thanks to a frequent train service. The plot, whose presence shocked Shaw, is in fact tightly controlled, and functions through strictly limited physical means, notably the crucial handbag, with Jack's cigarette case and the Army Lists in support. (A comparison with the four-act version is interesting in this connection; for this final scene Wilde supplies Dr Chasuble with a railway guide, Cecily with a *History of Our Own Times*, Miss Prism with price lists of the Civil Service Stores and Lady Bracknell with a copy of *The Green Carnation*.) The characters belong to traditional categories: there are two pairs of young 'romantic' lovers; a pair of older 'grotesques'; a pair of separated orphan brothers; a 'blocking' parent. The perfection of the resolution has only one minor blemish, the fact that Algernon remains in need of re-christening, but this passes unnoticed in the theatre. The sense of pattern and balance is everywhere apparent, from the matching of the cucumber sandwiches with the muffins to the verbal duets between Cecily and Gwendolen, and between Algernon and Jack.

122

Indeed, one possible criticism is that Wilde's use of such patterns and elements runs the risk of seeming mechanical. Mary McCarthy, following Shaw in her reservations, even uses the word 'tedium' of the second act:

The joke of gluttony and the joke of rudeness (which are really the same one, for heartlessness is the basic pleasantry) have been exhausted in the first act: nothing can be said by the muffin that has not already been said by the cucumber sandwich.[6]

If the joke was simply gluttony, there might be some force in the complaint. Mary McCarthy, perhaps abetted by the style of the production she was responding to, has coarsened Wilde's intentions, one of which was surely to disconcert his audience by presenting them with a distorted image of the conventions of leisured society. The tea ceremony is first parodied by Algernon eating all the cucumber sandwiches in advance (though, as it happens, Lady Bracknell has already satisfied herself with crumpets). The Hertfordshire tea is doubly exploited, initially as the mock-heroic weapons with which Cecily and Gwendolen duel:

GWENDOLEN: You have filled my tea with lumps of sugar, and though I asked most distinctly for bread and butter, you have given me cake. I am known for the gentleness of my disposition, and the extraordinary sweetness of my nature, but I warn you, Miss Cardew, you may go too far.

CECILY [*rising*]: To save my poor, innocent, trusting boy from the machinations of any other girl there are no lengths to which I would not go.[7]

Algernon's muffin-eating comes as an extension, and a contrasting extension, of the joke. John Gielgud realised only towards the end of his career that the muffin-eating should be played slowly, 'with real solemnity': 'you must not indulge yourself, or caricature'.[8] Wilde's artifice is so subtle that one hesitates to labour a point in commenting on it; but slow, deliberate muffin-eating is surely the appropriate style, so that it becomes a superbly insouciant, even impertinent, act, the dramatic equivalent of Wilde addressing the St James's audience cigarette in hand. In order to mock materialism without seeming to, Wilde raises, through Algernon, the most common action to a fine art:

JACK: How you can sit there, calmly eating muffins when we are in this horrible trouble, I can't make out. You seem to me to be perfectly heartless.

ALGERNON: Well, I can't eat muffins in an agitated manner. The butter would probably get on my cuffs. One should always eat muffins quite calmly. It is the only way to eat them.[9]

The 'trivial', 'heartless' muffin-eating acts as counterpoint to the situation, and to the discussion of the 'serious' problems that apparently prevent Algernon's and Jack's marriages to Cecily and Gwendolen, the arrangements for the dual christening and the predicaments of the fictional Bunbury and Ernest. Algernon's attitude is shown to be the only possible response – 'the most wonderful Bunbury I have ever had in my life'. Jack is temporarily disconcerted; a moment later he has repossessed the muffin dish, and instinctively followed Algernon's example: 'I suppose a man may eat his own muffins in his own garden.' It is his salvation. From the girls' perspective, looking out into the garden from within the house at the start of the last act: 'They have been eating muffins. That looks like repentance.'[10]

The muffin-eating, then, is not extraneous, a one-paced, repetitive, farcical joke: it is a gestural counterpoint to the sentimental affairs of the heart which form the largely unspoken structure within the sequence. This playful exploitation of social convention is repeated frequently by Wilde in his use of, and quotation of, dramatic convention, from romantic comedy, farce and melodrama. Jack's approach to Miss Prism is a striking example:

JACK [*in a pathetic voice*]: Miss Prism, more is restored to you than this handbag. I was the baby you placed in it.
MISS PRISM [*amazed*]: You?
JACK [*embracing her*]: Yes . . . mother!
MISS PRISM [*recoiling in indignant astonishment*]: Mr Worthing, I am unmarried!
JACK: Unmarried! I do not deny that is a serious blow. But after all, who has the right to cast a stone against one who has suffered? Cannot repentance wipe out an act of folly? Why should there be one law for men, and another for women? Mother, I forgive you.
[*Tries to embrace her again*]
MISS PRISM [*still more indignant*]: Mr. Worthing, there is some error. [*Pointing to Lady Bracknell*] There is the lady who can tell you who you really are.
JACK [*after a pause*]: Lady Bracknell, I hate to seem inquisitive, but would you kindly inform me who I am?[11]

Jack falls into one pose, adjusts rapidly in the light of Miss Prism's indignation, adopts an equally well-known variation, and moves unconcernedly on. The characters display a remarkable ability to adjust their attitude to fit the facts, or the facts to fit their attitude. Wilde seems here to be mocking the content of *A Woman of No Importance* as much as the conventions of melodrama; he is able to do it lightly and swiftly and without interference to the tone of *The Importance of Being Earnest*.

By his command of language, Wilde achieved a unity that he had accomplished only, among his plays, with *Salomé*. Whatever one's opinion of the success of the three 'modern' comedies, it is impossible to ignore an intermittent unevenness, caused by the clash between the 'serious' and the 'trivial'. In *The Importance of Being Earnest*, Wilde maintains a contrast between Algernon and Jack, a contrast complicated by Jack's assumption of a mask on his trips to town; but that contrast is subsumed within a shared use of language – a register that has already been unfolded in the exchanges between Algernon and his manservant Lane. A pair of witty young men is not unexpected; less predictable is the way in which first the hitherto silent Gwendolen, and in Act Two the supposedly naive Cecily, express themselves in such a sharp and distinctive mode. The second main register belongs to Lady Bracknell, who erupts into the play with a use of words as original and disconcerting as her attitudes. The third register, that of Canon Chasuble and Miss Prism, offers a delightful contrast, with its mixture of pedantic precept and idiosyncratic diversion. Their response to the visual humour of Jack's arrival in deepest mourning is an instance of how Wilde's linguistic invention extends and develops the initial joke:

CHASUBLE: Dear Mr Worthing, I trust this garb of woe does not betoken some terrible calamity?
JACK: My brother.
MISS PRISM: More shameful debts and extravagance?
CHASUBLE: Still leading his life of pleasure?
JACK [*shaking his head*]: Dead!
CHASUBLE: Your brother Ernest dead?
JACK: Quite dead.
MISS PRISM: What a lesson for him! I trust he will profit by it.[12]

Throughout, Wilde's familiar paradoxes and epigrams make a substantial contribution. But the verbal wit is of many kinds and one needs to return to Congreve, or look forward to the versatility of Stoppard, to find a text so consistently interesting to the ear.

OSCAR WILDE

For all its elegance of construction and linguistic polish, the play also contrives to have a sense of leisure. Its fringes are peopled with minor off-stage characters, who serve not only to delight and divert but also to relate the fictional world to the real. There are, for example, the society ladies whom Lady Bracknell cites: Lady Harbury, looking twenty years younger since her poor husband's death; Mary Farquhar, who flirts with her own husband across the dinner-table; the dear Duchess of Bolton. There are, too, the significantly absent Victorian fathers: Lord Bracknell, the late Mr Thomas Cardew, and poor Jenkins the carter, unfortunate father of twins. These, like the off-stage characters in Gogol's *The Government Inspector*, are given such definition by Wilde's descriptions that they seem constantly on the point of joining the action, fleetingly glimpsed reflections of the stage world Wilde has called into being.

A second series of contacts with a world outside the perfect artificiality of Wilde's creation is formed by the references to everyday life. One of these is, appropriately, central to the plot: the cloakroom at Victoria station. Some of these references are simply signposts: The Albany, Tunbridge Wells, Worthing, Willis's, the Empire; others are more concrete, initially reassuring, but cumulatively faintly disconcerting, as the customs and etiquette of Victorian social life are parodied and distorted: the visit from an aunt, the proposal, the economics lesson under the yew-tree, the diary entries of a Victorian lady.

Beneath the external politeness, the major principle which motivates each character is a pronounced ruthlessness in pursuit of his or her desire. For the lovers, the object of their quest is naturally the preferred partner, though for Gwendolen and Cecily the loved one is an idealised image, or mask, named Ernest, whom the heroes strive to impersonate. (The effect is somewhat as if, in a Shakespearean comedy, disguise should convey the true character.) These quests send Jack to London, ostensibly in search of his wicked younger brother, Algernon Bunburying to Hertfordshire, and Gwendolen on an unchaperoned expedition to the country; while Cecily, guarded by Miss Prism, is compelled to conduct both sides of her love affair within the pages of her own diary. (The fictional diary, like the three-volume novel and indeed the play itself, challenges and overcomes the less satisfying facts of 'reality'.) To accomplish their desires, Jack is prepared to kill his brother, and Algernon Bunbury, and both submit to the prospect of a ritual death by drowning in baptism, while Cecily and

126

Gwendolen do battle with cake-slice and sugar-tongs within the tea ceremony. The suppressed intensity of sexual appetite is echoed by the way the characters lay waste large quantities of food and drink. Algernon and Jack demolish most of the tea before Lady Bracknell arrives, already fed on crumpets, and move on to the sherry decanter after her departure; Cecily presses cake and sugared tea on Gwendolen; Algernon defies Jack over the muffins, while off-stage the champagne disappears at a brisk rate. Only the comparatively brief Act Three lacks refreshment, bar the catalogue of Jack's excesses and the intrusion of the temperance beverage which exploded in the handbag at Leamington. By then, though, the lovers have each other to distract them.

Lady Bracknell's purpose, though vicarious, is of a piece with that of the quartet of lovers: to find a suitable match for Gwendolen, and to monitor her nephew's activities. like the Duchess of Berwick, she allows nothing to divert her from her objective, even descending to the purchase of information by means of a small coin and entrusting herself, like a parcel, to a luggage train. Her principles, though she pays verbal respect to family and position, rest firmly on money, in large quantities and for preference in the funds. Her own marriage established the tradition:

When I married Lord Bracknell I had no fortune of any kind. But I never dreamed for a moment of allowing that to stand in my way.[13]

The preceding line, 'But I do not approve of mercenary marriages', marks yet one more assertion of practice over precept, as does Chasuble's abandonment of celibacy for the mature charms of Miss Prism.

The pre-eminence of the material, which embraces this suppression of social and moral convention to the satisfaction of desire, is exemplified by the play's central image, the handbag, in which the baby was substituted for the manuscript of that three-volume novel 'of more than revolting sentimentality'. When the magic object is triumphantly produced, there can be no sense of surprise that Miss Prism's first thought is for the restoration of her possession:

It has been a great inconvenience being without it all these years.[14]

rather than an answer to Lady Bracknell's imperious question, 'Where is that baby?' By this juncture, the comic, reversed world has been irrevocably established as the norm.

The discovery, first of Jack's identity and secondly of his name, completes the pattern. Throughout the play Wilde's characters have been striving single-mindedly to construct an idealised world which satisfies equally their wishes and their sense of form. If necessary, Lady Bracknell is prepared to change both the location of Jack's town house in Berkeley Square, and the fashion. The desired form may be a question of nomenclature (Egeria, Ernest) or of behaviour (wickedness), but it is invariably one of expression. As Gwendolen reminds Cecily, 'In matters of grave importance, style, not sincerity, is the vital thing.'[15] The dandiacal style of this idealised world requires that Jack be Ernest; and by the grace of Wilde and the Army Lists, he is and always has been Ernest. Fact is happily subservient to Fiction, Life is made to imitate Art: the predominance of Form is absolute.

It is not difficult to understand how critics like Shaw and Mary McCarthy were repelled by the play's coldness:

Clever as it was, it was his first really heartless play. In the others the chivalry of the eighteenth century Irishman and the romance of the disciple of Théophile Gautier (Oscar was really old-fashioned in the Irish way, except as a critic of morals) not only gave a certain kindness and gallantry to the serious passages and to the handling of women, but provided that proximity of emotion without which laughter, however irresistible, is destructive and sinister. In *The Importance of Being Earnest* this had vanished; and the play, though extremely funny, was essentially hateful.[16]

In *The Importance of Being Earnest* the 'serious' passages, in the conventional sense, are not present at all; as for the 'proximity of emotion', Shaw presumably means emotion that is articulated through language, emotion that is indicated by the form and tone of what a character says. The emotion that *The Importance of Being Earnest* is primarily concerned with is love; and Wilde does not indicate it explicitly because it is implicit in the form he has chosen, which deliberately echoes, as well as parodies, the patterns and conventions of romantic comedy. The characters, with the exception of Lady Bracknell, are motivated by love: a particularly instinctive, irrational and inexplicable kind of love, apparently incompatible with the demands and restriction of society, which is finally endorsed by the fictive *dénouement* and, miraculously, richly blessed by the required norms, good birth and ample wealth. This kind of affirmation through dramatic form is often at odds with, or at least in complex relation to, the purely verbal text. The unresolved ambivalence in Orsino's rapid avowal to Viola in *Twelfth Night*, or Hero's acceptance of Claudio in *Much Ado about Nothing*, indicate the kind of tension that is discernible, but more widespread, within *The Importance of Being Earnest*. In Shakespearean or, indeed, Restoration Comedy, the unspoken, the sub-text which is largely conveyed by visual means, is usually clarified and validated by one particular exchange when the masks are put aside and the truths of the heart are revealed. The confession of love between Benedick and Beatrice is an example of such a scene, or the half-dreaming affirmations of the lovers in *A Midsummer Night's Dream* after Theseus's departure. But the absence of such an exchange does not necessarily imply the absence of emotion. Part of Shaw's reservations may have been exacerbated by the style of acting in the first production: he thought the actors 'insufferably affected', and even George Alexander, as Jack, rushed through the third act. No doubt such affectation and contrived pace nourished the sense of 'Gilbertian extravagance' which reviewers identified in the production: it is a style of acting at odds with Wilde's unusual kind of comedy, which requires sincerity. The 'heart', in fact, is a constituent of the form, part of the 'trivial' world of play and artifice which sweeps up not only the two pairs of lovers but also the celibate guardians of Victorian moral values, Canon Chasuble and Miss Prism.

Shaw was right in noting that *The Importance of Being Earnest* marked a change in Wilde's mode of writing; but it was a development rather than a regression. As Katharine Worth has commented, with this play 'Wilde anticipated a major development in the twentieth century, the use of farce to make fundamentally serious (not earnest!) explorations in the realm of the irrational'.[17] While Wilde's underlying generosity and warmth surface at the play's conclusion, the cumulative effect of language and action is to function as a subversive critique of Victorian attitudes and institutions, all the more telling for being so lightly elegant in expression. It is the hypocrisy of society that Wilde aims at, for instance the notion that marriage is an ideal state. This idea is exploded regularly throughout the play, starting with the first exchanges between Algernon and Lane:

ALGERNON: Why is it that at a bachelor's establishment the servants invariably drink the champagne? I ask merely for information.

LANE: I attribute it to the superior quality of the wine, sir. I have often observed that in married households the champagne is rarely of a first-rate brand.[18]

The development of the idea, however, introduces one of those disconcerting glimpses of Victorian reality which protrude momentarily into the artistic luxury of the play-world:

ALGERNON: Good heavens! Is marriage so demoralizing as that?
LANE: I believe it *is* a very pleasant state, sir. I have had very little experience of it myself up to the present. I have only been married once. That was in consequence of a misunderstanding between myself and a young person.
ALGERNON [*languidly*]: I don't know that I am much interested in your family life, Lane.
LANE: No, sir; it is not a very interesting subject. I never think of it myself.

This *exposé* of marriage, for which the later references to Lord Bracknell provide a regular reminder, leads to Algernon's paradoxical complaint:

ALGERNON: Lane's views on marriage seem somewhat lax. Really, if the lower orders don't set us a good example, what on earth is the use of them? They seem, as a class, to have absolutely no sense of moral responsibility.[19]

The comment is not extended – nothing in this play is laboured – but the motif of the potential instability of the class system is picked up by further oblique references. Lady Bracknell, while condemning the theory of modern education as 'radically unsound', finds good reason to be thankful:

Fortunately in England, at any rate, education produces no effect whatsoever. If it did, it would prove a serious danger to the upper classes, and probably lead to acts of violence in Grosvenor Square.[20]

More striking, because of the context, is the bizarre, almost absurdist, comparison which comes to her mind on the revelation of Jack's origins:

To be born, or at any rate bred, in a hand-bag, whether it had handles or not, seems to me to display a contempt for the ordinary decencies of family life that reminds me of the worst excesses of the French Revolution. And I presume you know what that unfortunate movement led to?[21]

Lady Bracknell, the self-appointed guardian of society as well as of Gwendolen, is pathologically sensitive about potential disturbances to its equilibrium:

Exploded! Was he the victim of a revolutionary outrage? I was not aware that Mr Bunbury was interested in social legislation. If so, he is well punished for his morbidity.[22]

To note this sequence of passing, exquisitely phrased references is not to suggest that Wilde is undertaking a systematic, satirical *exposé* of society. Their importance is that, cumulatively, they provide an almost subliminal reminder of the central lies on which Victorian and most other societies are founded, wholly in tune with the subversive impact of the play's action. The heartlessness Shaw saw in *The Importance of Being Earnest* is the heartlessness Wilde saw in the modern world: a sense of void expressed in other plays as diverse in method as those of Beckett and Stoppard. Stoppard's use of *The Importance of Being Earnest* in *Travesties* is, among other things, a recognition of the play's centrality, and a reminder that the intellectual and the artificial are compatible with emotion.

9

De Profundis and *The Ballad of Reading Gaol*

De Profundis was the title given by Robert Ross to the extract, less than half of Wilde's original manuscript, which he published in 1905. There was no indication at that time that the work was in the form of a letter to Lord Alfred Douglas. The letter was written by Wilde during the first three months of 1897, and the manuscript is described in some detail by Rupert Hart-Davis in *Letters*.[1] It was, in spite of its literary tone, a letter which Wilde intended to send: 'As regards your letter to me in answer to this, it may be as long or as short as you choose. Address the envelope to "The Governor, H.M. Prison, Reading".'[2] It is hard to imagine a reply which would have satisfied Wilde; Douglas spent much of the rest of his life attempting to respond. The Prison Commission refused permission for the letter to be sent, so it was handed to Wilde on his release from Reading on 18 May 1897. When Wilde reached Dieppe on 20 May, he entrusted the letter to Ross. He had previously written to Ross, when he still presumed he would be able to send *De Profundis* from prison, in terms which help to define the nature of this remarkable work, and which give some inkling as to Wilde's motives.

In Wilde's letter of 1 April 1897, he asks Ross to have the letter copied, 'As soon as you, and of course More Adey whom I always include with you, have read it . . .'[3] If Ross is to be his literary executor, he must be 'in possession of the only document that really gives any explanation of my extraordinary behaviour with regard to Queensberry and Alfred Douglas'. The letter is, first, intended to give a psychological explanation of his course of conduct: 'I don't defend my conduct, I explain it.' Secondly, the letter contains passages which deal with Wilde's 'mental development in prison', and which will help his friends understand 'in what mood and manner' Wilde hoped to face the world. Thirdly, the letter is designed to do Douglas good: 'It is the first time anyone has ever told him the truth about himself.' Lastly, in terms of Wilde's expressed intentions, the process of writing, of finding expression and utterance, enabled him to cleanse his 'bosom of much perilous stuff', ridding himself of a 'growing burden of bitterness'.

Included in the letter to Ross were highly explicit instructions about copying *De Profundis*:

> I wish the copy to be done not on tissue paper but on good paper such as is used for plays, and a wide rubricated margin should be left for corrections. The copy done and verified from the manuscript, the original should be despatched to A. D. by More, and another copy done by the typewriter so that *you* should have a copy as well as myself.[4]

Wilde also gave instructions for copies to be made of selected passages and sent to two women friends. In the event, Ross sent Douglas a typed copy (which Douglas denied receiving), kept the second, and in 1909 gave the manuscript to the British Museum on condition that it was not to be unsealed for fifty years.

De Profundis was, from the start, in some sense both personal and public. It was Wilde writing to (and for) Douglas; to his close friends; to and for himself. Undoubtedly, in view both of the form and content of the letter and his plans for its immediate copying, Wilde anticipated the possibility that it might, in whole or in part, be put before a wider public as an essay in literary autobiography.

In organisation, it falls into three parts. The first (approximately pages 873–912 in *Works*) is concerned with an inquisition into Douglas's conduct, and an explanation of Wilde's. Autobiographically, this long section is of great interest, since it provides a detailed account of the impact of Douglas's friendship on Wilde's life and art before the trials, an explanation of Wilde's conduct during the three trials, and some insight into Wilde's mental and physical state during the period of his imprisonment. In the central section (which forms the major proportion of the extract Ross published) Wilde shifts overtly to self-analysis, after expressing the need to forgive Douglas and the admission that he ruined himself. Beginning with the startling retrospective summary, 'I was a man who stood in symbolic relations to the art and culture of my age', Wilde proceeds to create a new self-image with which to encounter the world on his imminent release. While the first section is dominated by the idea of Pleasure, the second is a response to Pain; and these two motifs, with their corresponding Comic and Tragic Masks, form the controlling contraries of the work. Whereas the first phase recalls Wilde as a social being, the second emphasises his heroic isolation through an extended comparison with the life and suffering of Christ, who becomes the archetype of the Individualist and the first Romantic artist. The third section returns to the manner of the first, though now

Douglas's mother receives a portion of blame, perhaps as a representative of the forces of society which have rejected Wilde; while Douglas is characterised as having acted like Rosencrantz and Guildenstern to Wilde's Hamlet ('There is a wide difference between you. What with them was chance, with you was choice').[5] This last section (from page 937 or so in *Works*), though its emotional intensity seems at first dissipated by the resumption of a petulance one might have assumed had been exorcised, constitutes a terrible reminder of the particular nature of Wilde's tragic fall. The society which has punished Wilde so fiercely remains collectively vindictive. The artistic soul 'pour qui le monde visible existe' will have to contend with Philistine and Pharisee.

Much of the poignancy of *De Profundis* derives from our accumulated knowledge about Wilde's ruin. It is the statement that Wilde did not make from the witness-box; and his apologia appears even more persuasive with the passing of time. The picture, however partial, that we receive of Victorian society is chilling enough. The description of Wilde's infatuation with Douglas, and the intellectually and imaginatively sterile nature of their relationship, has tragic overtones. The overtones are Wilde's; he does not spare Douglas either in his selection of incident or in his handling of it; but neither does he spare himself, and as the catalogue of pettiness unrolls, one may discern that Wilde is delineating a mask that he has experimented with and is now theoretically ready to discard: the mask of superficiality, of trivial pleasure. Certainly, through Wilde's treatment in *De Profundis*, the triviality is made to appear highly unappealing. The roll-call of luncheons at the Café Royal, dinners at Voisin's or the Savoy, suppers at Paillard's or Wilton's, have a joyless feel, weighed down by the ominous reminder of their cost – 'My expenses for eight days in Paris for myself, you, and your Italian servant were nearly £150: Paillard alone absorbing £85.'[6] The near farce of Douglas's influenza at the Grand Hotel, Brighton followed by Wilde's in his Worthing lodgings furnished with stage properties of lemonade, telegrams and dinner-knife, has all the in-dignity of a shrill suburban quarrel. (It is interesting to compare Wilde's retrospective treatment of these weeks with the impression conveyed by his letters written at the time, and, indeed, with their comic transformation as the Bunbury double-life in *The Importance of being Earnest*.) Wilde clearly wishes to establish the theme of sorrow which lay close to the surface even during the pleasant passages of his time with Douglas – 'as though my life, whatever it had seemed to myself and to others, had all the while been a real Symphony of Sorrow, passing through its rhythmically-linked movements to its certain resolution, with that inevitableness that in Art characterises the treatment of every great theme'.[7] By rejecting the life of pleasure, Wilde prepares the way for a new baptism into his role of suffering Artist. It is the denial of his own vocation which forms Wilde's major self-accusation:

I blame myself for allowing an unintellectual friendship, a friendship whose primary aim was not the creation and contemplation of beautiful things, to entirely dominate my life . . . You did not realise that an artist, and especially such an artist as I am, one, that is to say, the quality of whose work depends on the intensification of personality, requires for the development of his art the companionship of ideas, and intellectual atmosphere, quiet, peace, and solitude.[8]

A further definition of Wilde's artistic dream refers to 'that beautiful unreal world of Art where once I was King, and would have remained King, indeed, had I not let myself be lured into the imperfect world of coarse uncompleted passions, of appetite without distinction, desire without limit, and formless greed'.[9]

Wilde's concept of the Artist is the central theme of *De Profundis*. It is the recurrent though often submerged subject of the first section, where Wilde probes his own betrayal of his sacred role. In the second, it bursts out in an astonishing, extravagant, but wholly serious claim:

I was a man who stood in symbolic relations to the art and culture of my age. I had realised this for myself at the very dawn of my manhood, and had forced my age to realise it afterwards. Few men hold such a position in their own lifetime and have it so acknowledged. It is usually discerned, if discerned at all, by the historian, or the critic, long after both the man and his age have passed away. With me it was different. I felt it by myself, and made others feel it. Byron was a symbolic figure, but his relations were to the passion of his age and its weariness of passion. Mine were to something more noble, more permanent, of more vital issue, of larger scope.

The gods had given me almost everything. I had genius, a distin-guished name, high social position, brilliancy, intellectual daring: I made art a philosophy, and philosophy an art: I altered the minds of men and the colours of things: there was nothing I said or did that did not make people wonder: I took the drama, the most objective form known to art, and made it as personal a mode of expression as the lyric or the sonnet, at the same time that I widened its range and enriched its characterisation: drama, novel, poem in rhyme, poem in prose, subtle or fantastic dialogue, whatever I touched I made beautiful in a new mode of beauty: to truth itself I gave what is false no less than what is true as its rightful province, and showed that the false and the true are merely forms of intellectual existence. I treated Art as the supreme reality, and life as a mere mode of fiction: I awoke the imagination of my century so that it created myth and legend around me: I summed up all systems in a phrase, and all existence in an epigram.[10]

The God-like figure whom Wilde has created (a kind of extension of Dorian Gray) possessed one major flaw. 'What the paradox was to me in the sphere of thought, perversity became to me in the sphere of passion . . . I was no longer the Captain of my Soul, and did not know it.'[11] Wilde turns to the only remedy, 'absolute Humility'; and positively embraces his suffering which he transforms into an idealised sorrow. He defines sorrow in terms of art. 'What the artist is always looking for is that mode of existence in which soul and body are one and indivisible: in which the outward is expressive of the inward: in which Form reveals.'[12] Sorrow has unity with itself: 'Pain, unlike Pleasure, wears no mask;' it is 'the ultimate type both in life and Art'.[13] Such a definition allows Wilde first to see each prisoner, including himself, in a special light, a living example of his recurrent idea of the criminal as hero: 'There is not a single wretched man in this wretched place along with me who does not stand in symbolic relations to the very secret of life.' It also leads to the development of the motif of the suffering servant of Isaiah, in Wilde's vision of Christ the Man of Sorrows as the type of the artist.

The comparisons Wilde makes between himself and Christ build on earlier references within his own work, in particular the treatment of suffering and sacrifice in 'The Happy Prince', 'The Nightingale and the Rose' and the stories in *A House of Pomegranates*. Wilde quotes Isaiah on the suffering servant: 'He is despised and rejected of men, a man of sorrows and acquainted with grief: and we hid as it were our faces from him.'[14] There is an obvious relevance for anyone in Wilde's circumstances, let alone someone as prone as he was to self-dramatisation. But the extension of the comparison to the figure of Christ himself is unexpected. It is implicit even in his description of Robert Ross gravely removing his hat as Wilde passed him on the way to the Court of Bankruptcy – ('It was in this spirit, and with this mode of love that the saints knelt down to wash the feet of the poor, or stooped to kiss the leper on the cheek')[15] – an incident which he presents in much the same terms as, later, he uses of Mary Magdalen breaking the alabaster vase of spices over Christ's feet. At other times, Wilde's imaginative references to the suffering of Christ recall the phrasing of a previous writer of letters from prison, Paul. The Bible is a constant influence on Wilde's writing; it is not surprising that, with Wilde deprived of his library, its presence becomes so marked in *De Profundis*.

Several aspects of Christ's life and teaching were especially apposite to Wilde: his opposition to the Pharisees, his use of the child as a model, his apparent predilection for the company of sinners. The major point of reference, however, is Wilde's perception of Christ as Romantic Artist, an extension or reinterpretation of his traditional title of Son of Man. Wilde had previously suggested connections between himself and a number of Romantic writers, notably Keats, Shelley, and Byron. The enlistment of Christ in the cause of Romanticism is one of his more innovative and suprising ideas.

Wilde does not record any leap of faith towards Christ, but provides a detailed account of a slow and individualistic approach to him. His references to Renan and Pater indicate an awareness that he is attempting a reinterpretation which many others in the second half of the nineteenth century were compelled to undertake. He disposes first of three traditional props of belief, Morality – he is antinomian; Religion – 'My Gods dwell in temples made with hands, and within the circle of actual experience is my creed made perfect and complete';[16] and Reason – which tells him that the laws under which he was convicted were wrong and unjust. His approach is based purely on his own experience: a perception that 'whatever is realised is right', and the insight that all experience, first the experience of self but also vicarious experience – because 'whatever happens to another happens to oneself' – may be accepted and transformed. The 'Soul, in its turn, has its nutritive functions also, and can transform into noble moods of thought, and passions of high import, what in itself is base, cruel, and degrading'.[17] The acceptance of Sorrow, and the discovery of Humility, are not seen as merely passive moods. Wilde emphasises the necessity of being happy, and of looking forward to new developments in Art and Life.

From this exposition of his present spiritual and mental state, one admittedly as yet untested but which is laid out with the pressure of life outside prison in mind, Wilde proceeds to depict the personality of Christ. Just as Christ, for Wilde, made a beautiful image for himself, the image of the Man of Sorrows, so Wilde's depiction is unmistakably interpretative, an artefact, rather than offered as historical or theological analysis. There are two main thrusts towards the presentation of Christ as Artist. The first is by emphasising the literary and poetical elements in the transmission of the myths about Christ, by referring to the Gospels as prose-poems, by describing Christ's life as poem, drama, idyll. The second, more radical, is to depict Christ as being essentially self-creating: 'out of his own imagination entirely did Jesus of Nazareth create himself'.[18] Wilde sees Christ as the first and supreme individualist, teaching not Philanthropy or Altruism (both briskly dismissed by Wilde in 'The Soul of Man Under Socialism') but the self-fulfilling doctrine that the Kingdom of God is within you. Christ's uniqueness lay in his ability, through an act of the imagination, to sympathise with others, and especially with sinners; thus he could express not just his own soul, but the soul of man. The imagination exercised in this way, Wilde argues, is 'simply a manifestation of Love, and it is love, and the capacity for it, that distinguishes one human being from another'.[19]

Two implications of Wilde's imitation of Christ invite comment. One is his focus on Christ and the sinner. He refers to Mary Magdalen, to the woman taken in adultery, and highlights Christ's sympathetic understanding of them. But he extends his sympathy into the sublimation of the sinner: 'Christ, through some divine instinct in him, seems to have always loved the sinner as being the nearest possible approach to the perfection of man . . . in a manner not yet understood of the world he regarded sin and suffering as being in themselves beautiful, holy things, and modes of perfection.' As though conscious of the implications of such an interpretation Wilde adds, 'It *sounds* a very dangerous idea. It is so.' Later in *De Profundis* Wilde offers an account of his own fascination with sinners:

People thought it dreadful of me to have entertained at dinner the evil things of life, and to have found pleasure in their company. But they, from the point of view through which I, as an artist in life, approach them, were delightfully suggestive and stimulating. It was like feasting with panthers. The danger was half the excitement. I used to feel as the snake-charmer must feel when he lures the cobra to stir from the painted cloth or reed-basket that holds it, and makes it spread its hood at his bidding, and sway to and fro in the air as a plant sways restfully in a stream. They were to me the brightest of gilded snakes. Their poison was part of their perfection.[20]

Wilde's preoccupation with 'sin', with the dark underlay to Victorian life, while not the key to *De Profundis*, is nevertheless an important motif which surfaces repeatedly. Significantly, the two subjects which Wilde proposed should he ever write again were 'Christ, as the precursor of the Romantic movement in life' and 'the Artistic life considered in its relation to Conduct'.[21]

The second implication relates to a development in Wilde's own thinking. Here, as so often, he takes up ideas and motifs from earlier work, and the Christ he invokes has already made an appearance in the closing pages of 'The Soul of Man under Socialism'. There, his Christ was already very much an individualist, but an isolated individualist, suffering, a God 'realizing his perfection through pain', and not concerned with 'the beauty of life and the joy of living'. For these, men had to wait for the Renaissance; and when it dawned, men could no longer understand Christ. Now, Wilde perceives a different pattern.

To me one of the things in history the most to be regretted is that the Christ's own renaissance which had produced the Cathedral of Chartres, the Arthurian cycle of legends, the life of St Francis of Assisi, the art of Giotto, and Dante's *Divine Comedy*, was not allowed to develop on its own lines but was interrupted and spoiled by the dreary classical Renaissance that gave us Petrarch, and Raphael's frescoes, and Palladian architecture, and formal French tragedy, and St. Paul's Cathedral, and Pope's poetry, and everything that is made from without and by dead rules, and does not spring from within through some spirit informing it. But wherever there is a romantic movement in Art, there somehow, and under some form, is Christ, or the soul of Christ.[22]

Wilde proceeds to attribute to the spirit of Christ his pantheon of artistic achievement: *Romeo and Juliet*, *La Belle Dame sans Merci*, *Les Fleurs du Mal*, the stained glass and tapestries and quattrocento work of Burne-Jones and Morris, Verlaine, 'and the love of children and flowers'. It is not a logical way of proceeding, but Wilde's sheer confidence in his aesthetic judgments and conviction about his theory create a powerful impact.

The first two parts of *De Profundis*, if one accepts the approximate division indicated above, are much more sharply organised than the third. The figure of Douglas (whether as an objective third person or a projection of Wilde) dominates the first, corresponding to the focus on the past, the world, pleasure, and the emotion of hate, while the contrasting figure of Christ controls the second, with the shift to the present, the spiritual, pain, and the emotion of love. The work seems poised for development, or

139

synthesis, in the concluding section, where the artist might ideally be shown emerging into some perfected state such as Wilde portrayed in *The Star-Child*, who passed through a phase of hard-hearted beauty succeeded by one of selfless suffering:

And they fell on his neck and kissed him, and brought him into the palace, and clothed him in fair raiment, and set the crown upon his head, and the sceptre in his hand, and over the city that stood by the river he ruled, and was its lord.[23]

In *De Profundis*, however, the third section fails to create an idealised future. Instead, Wilde returns for the most part to the bitter, often petulant, accusatory mode of the opening, with his re-cataloguing of the enormities of Douglas and his father, and his castigation of the mother's weakness. Wilde does indeed project a future meeting with Douglas, with changed names, in some idealised town abroad:

At the end of the month, when the June roses are in all their wanton opulence, I will, if I feel able, arrange through Robbie to meet you in some quiet foreign town like Bruges, whose grey houses and green canals and cool still ways had a charm for me, years ago.[24]

Such an encounter strikes a note of pathos after the earlier visions – 'Far off, like a perfect pearl, one can see the city of God.' Wilde's reiteration of the power of love lacks conviction:

to Humility there is nothing that is impossible, and to Love all things are easy.[25]

He recognises the imperfection, the incompletion, in his closing sentences:

How far I am away from the true temper of soul, this letter in its changing uncertain moods, its scorn and bitterness, its aspirations and its failure to realise those aspirations, shows you quite clearly.[26]

Wilde never revised *De Profundis* after he left prison, though Hart-Davis has argued that certain sheets of the manuscript 'have every appearance of being fair copies'. The work swings out of Wilde's artistic control into personal spontaneity; as he said of *The Ballad of Reading Gaol*, 'that it is interesting from more points of view than one is artistically to be regretted'.[27] However, the imperfectly exercised artistic control is, arguably, in the end more distinctive and revelatory, so that Wilde in *De Profundis* creates an imaginative experience which has a vivid particularity found nowhere else in his prose fiction.

In *De Profundis*, Wilde attempted to chart his future artistic course. In fact, the only new work that he accomplished after his release from prison on 19 May 1897 was *The Ballad of Reading Gaol*, a poem so unlike anything else that he had ever written that it might be momentarily mistaken for a new departure. It was composed at Berneval-sur-Mer in Normandy in the summer of 1897:

I am in my chalet, and am beginning work, but I find I can only work about an hour and a half at a time . . . I like what I have done very much, though it is a new style for me. I am out-Henleying Kipling![28]

The *Ballad* was published by Leonard Smithers in February 1897: the first six editions gave the author as 'C.3.3', but there can have been little mystery about his identity. The poem is long (109 stanzas), repetitive, uneven, both rough and contrived in places, and undeniably powerful. Even Henley, who would not have appreciated anything in the nature of imitation by Wilde, admitted that 'sincerity, veracity, vision even, have their part in this mixty-maxty of differences'.[29] The ballad stanza which Wilde chose occurs in *The Rime of the Ancient Mariner*, and is that used by Hood for *The Dream of Eugene Aram*, another poem about a murderer, but one conceived wholly in terms of the murderer's guilt:

> Two sudden blows with a ragged stick,
> And one with a heavy stone,
> One hurried gash with a hasty knife, –
> And then the deed was done:
> There was nothing lying at my foot
> But lifeless flesh and bone![30]

Wilde's poem has a much more complex purpose and organisation than Hood's, in that the murderer is observed by another prisoner, and the poem moves between the various stages of the condemned man's progress towards the gallows – the pre-trial remand, the appearance in the dock, the condemned cell, the day of the hanging – and the reaction of the other prisoners, while a final section shifts the implications towards the common guilt of all men. It must be admitted that such a scheme is not consistently apparent, and that Wilde does not seem to be wholly in control of his material, in the way that we have become accustomed to in his previous work. As he admitted to Robert Ross, 'The poem suffers under the difficulty of a divided aim in style. Some is realistic, some romantic: some poetry, some propaganda. I feel it keenly, but as a whole I think the production interesting: that it is interesting from more points of view than one is artistically to be regretted.'[31]

OSCAR WILDE

It is the 'realistic' parts which tended to strike contemporary
reviewers most forcibly – stanzas with the raw specificity of this:

> We tore the tarry rope to shreds
> With blunt and bleeding nails;
> We rubbed the doors, and scrubbed the floors,
> And cleaned the shining rails:
> And, rank by rank, we soaped the plank,
> And clattered with the pails.

But again and again Wilde prepares for the wider implications by
more generalised yet savage irony:

> The Governor was strong upon
> The Regulations Act:
> The Doctor said that Death was but
> A Scientific fact:
> And twice a day the Chaplain called,
> And left a little tract.[32]

Henley criticised a later stanza for not being 'observed':

> The warders stripped him of his clothes
> And gave him to the flies;
> They marked the swollen, purple throat
> And the stark and staring eyes,
> And with laughter loud they heaped the shroud
> In which the convict lies.

'And how does the writer know that the warders trampled down
the poor devil's grave "with laughter loud"?'[33] But it is just this
kind of extension which gives the poem its force, as the criminal
becomes victim, a modern Christ-figure crucified by society, and
a symbol, first for the artist/outcast/criminal who is Wilde, but
also for the 'obscure deaths of the heart, the unseen violence upon
souls'. The poem is, among other things, a plea for prison reform,
in a different mode from Wilde's letters to the Daily Chronicle.
Arthur Symons wrote of 'its relative value in a career which may
now be at a turning point'.[34] With hindsight, one may see that
Wilde was too bruised by the reality of his prison experiences to
continue to develop his intellectual life, an intellect, as Yeats
described it, which 'had given itself to pure contemplation', and
'played with the fundamental and the insoluble'.[35]

10

Conclusion

There are several obstacles to be surmounted before coming to a conclusion about Wilde's achievement and about his importance as an artist. Two particular difficulties arise from the circumstances and after-effects of his trials and conviction. First, it is virtually impossible, and arguably inappropriate, to approach Wilde's work without some intervening biographical, or even moral, perspective. This may tend retrospectively to enhance, or conceivably devalue, the works one is responding to. The problem is common enough; but if one thinks of a spectrum stretching between writers about whom we know very little biographically, and might wish to know more (such as Shakespeare), and those about whom we are over-supplied with information (Virginia Woolf, Joe Orton), Wilde belongs in the outer reaches of the latter. There is a pull towards seeing Wilde's work as somehow explained or decoded by what was 'revealed' at and after his trial.

The second difficulty arises from the traumatic interruption which the trials caused to the development of Wilde's work. While naturally subject to chance and to the usual kinds of financial and psychological pressures, Wilde was a highly self-conscious artist who can be seen as conducting a systematic exploration of his role. The last few years of his active writing life were astonishingly fecund, especially in drama, where *Salomé* and *The Importance of Being Earnest* constitute two original and distinct achievements. The abrupt change of direction signalled by *De Profundis*, and the potentially radical reappraisal of himself as artist which it contains, leave one's assessment of Wilde's development in disarray. The idea of order which was implicit in all of Wilde's work hitherto is replaced by the human and affecting sense of chaos that emanates from Wilde's post-trial years. Wilde's attempts to recreate himself, and the retrospective self-criticism within *De Profundis*, induce awkward reflection on the relationship between art and society; and society's various rejections of Wilde's work – from the predictable censoring of *Salomé* to the long period of public hostility to anything associated with him – complicate and blur our perception. Wilde's unusual status, as both cult and

143

taboo figure, has deflected attention away from his writing. For instance, it is only comparatively recently that critical editions of selected individual works have become readily available.

In spite of these barriers Wilde challenges and invites one to formulate judgments, in part because his works and personality mock the commentator from behind a shifting display of masks, in part because of the very diversity of critical reaction which he has occasioned. George Moore, admittedly a far from objective critic, rated Wilde as 'in the third or fourth class, and, therefore, not worth troubling about, and I do not think that anybody would have troubled about him if the Marquess of Queensberry had not written him a post-card'.[1] There has to be a particular kind of quality which occasions dismissal on this scale and intensity, or the admiration which has also been afforded to him by figures such as Borges. There are equally divergent opinions about even his most widely acknowledged works. *Salomé* one might expect to arouse antipathy as well as enthusiasm; but it is slightly surprising to encounter dismissals of *The Importance of Being Earnest* by critics as witty and sensitive as Shaw or Mary McCarthy. Holbrook Jackson, in what still reads as one of the most balanced and perceptive judgments of Wilde, analyses the nature of the problem:

as the incidents associated with the life and times of Wilde recede further into the background of the mental picture which inevitably forms itself about any judgment of his work, we shall be able to obtain a less biased view. Even then, our perspective may be wrong, for this difficulty of personality is not only dominant, but it may be essential.[2]

The personality of Wilde was diffused throughout his works, and the problem of their tone, and of the level of their seriousness, confronts one continually.

The two most common kinds of approach towards critical assessment of Wilde might be described as the restrictive and the holistic. One form of the restrictive places Wilde as an artist of the Decadence, of the *fin-de-siècle*. The assumption by the popular press that the yellow-backed novel carried by Wilde at the time of his arrest was the 'Yellow Book' is the kind of fictional detail which encourages such a view, as does the association between Wilde's Salomé and Beardsley's illustrations. The connotations are, at best, unhealthy, at worst, obscene; and the style, of such ostensibly decadent works as *The Picture of Dorian Gray* or *Salomé* or a poem like 'The Harlot's House', is frequently dismissed as derivative, over-decorative and weary. However, one of the most remarkable features of Wilde in the early nineties is the vitality and variety of his output. It is, of course, unusual in English literature to have a writer with at least claims to be taken seriously who was at the same time a demonstrably popular playwright; to be a Decadent artist would seem in England to bring total disqualification. The traditional way round such a block, if it is even recognised, is to dismiss the popular plays as pastiches, money-spinners which Wilde himself did not take seriously. The curious fact about the three social comedies, as well as *The Importance of Being Earnest*, is the continued interest they hold for actors, directors and audiences: an interest which is substantially founded upon their unusual and elusive style.

Extreme eclecticism is inappropriate with so versatile a writer as Wilde; in fact, he conducted his own process of selection and refinement, mining his own writing for phrases and epigrams, or polishing his technique in, for example, the reworked artificiality of *The Sphinx*. The holistic approach, which sees him as positively indivisible from his works, and as having to a large extent fulfilled his claim to have stood 'in symbolic relations' to the art and culture of his age, is infinitely more fruitful. John Cowper Powys, for example, considered it a mistake to regard *De Profundis* as a recantation: 'It is a fulfilment, a completion, a rounding off. Like a black and a scarlet thread running through the whole tapestry of his tragic story are the two parallel "motifs", the passion of the beauty which leads to destruction and the passion of the beauty which leads to life.'[3] The most closely argued and persuasive modern reading of Wilde is by Rodney Shewan, who introduces *De Profundis* as bringing 'Wilde's artistic career full circle', and comments in his book's concluding paragraph: 'the fact that Wilde's life, his "gallant attempt to teach Nature her proper place", eventually took on so "deficient" a form, may well be his aptest symbolic achievement'.[4]

While recognising the essential unity of Wilde's life and work, the image of the circle deflects us from responding to the sense of potential, or innovation and experiment, which is found in the writings of his last creative years. One must somehow circum-navigate, while not ignoring, *De Profundis* and *The Ballad of Reading Gaol*, which Wilde has placed at the conclusion of the sequence, a position which seems to signal finality, the defeat of a lifetime's artistic endeavour, even, symbolically, the extinction of the Romantic impulse. Wilde participated fully in the nineteenth-century search for absolutes; prevented by social pressures of the most crushing kind from pursuing his search in art, it comes as no surprise to find him being received into the Roman Catholic Church in his dying moments. To treat art with the intellectual and moral seriousness of religion is one of the marks of Wilde's modernity. The belief in renewal and transformation breaks through the consciousness of something coming to an end.

The intensity of Wilde's absorption in art gives his work an unusual kind of purity. Borges, contrasting Wilde with Chesterton, described the former as 'a man who keeps an invulnerable innocence in spite of the habits of evil and misfortune'.[5] The idea of the child is an important one within Wilde's writings: transparently in the stories; in the figure of Dorian Gray, his beauty frozen on the brink of experience; in Salomé, half-child and half-woman; in the hard-edged idyll of The Importance of Being Earnest. The sense of innocence is largely a product of Wilde's style, founded upon simplicity of syntax, partly a product of his classical education, partly achieved by conscious effort and refinement, with the example of his master Flaubert before him. The lucidity of Wilde's style is commoner in French than in English. The Goncourts recorded Gautier's claims that his syntax was 'very tidily arranged' in his head: 'I throw my sentences into the air, like so many cats, and I know that they'll fall on their feet. It's all very simple: all you need is a good grasp of syntax.'[6] The simplicity came as a result of extended practice. No doubt Wilde's role as a professional conversationalist, or discourser and narrator, contributed signficantly to the development of his literary style. Yeats commented that he had never before heard anyone talking in perfect sentences, and praised Wilde as the greatest talker of his time; but he also suggested that the further he went in his writings from the method of speech, the less original he was. An alternative view would be to see the qualities and originality of Wilde's spoken methods as permeating and defining his written style. The lightness, the air of the ephemeral, the clarity which are widely characteristic of Wilde commend him more readily to the general reader than to the literary critic; as Borges notes, Wilde's 'perfection has been a disadvantage: his work is so harmonious that it may seem inevitable and even trite'.[7]

The voice of the author, and more especially the author's speaking voice, is one aspect of Wilde's modernity. His writings form an extended series of dramatic monologues. This is more obvious in the case of the lectures, essays and tales, or the epistolary form and style of *De Profundis*, than in the social comedies, which have the appearance of objectivity; but with the passage of time their strength can be seen to lie in the distinctiveness of their verbal and visual style. A remark like Henry James's about *Lady Windermere's Fan*, 'There is of course absolutely no characterisation and all the people talk equally strained Oscar',[8] betrays a relentlessly naturalistic and old-fashioned notion of character, made more apparent if one replaces Oscar with the name of Beckett or Pinter. The idea of a play as a transparent window through which to peer into life is one which Wilde merely toyed with, part of an elaborate transaction between him and his audience. The sense of play, indeed, is yet another significant aspect of Wilde as modernist. The potential importance of play is indicated by the very concept of life imitating art; and the idea that serious art inhabits territory situated on the borders of farce, a characteristic of modernism, is implied by much of Wilde's earlier writings and manner, before its crystallisation in *The Importance of Being Earnest*.

Wilde, the most versatile and representative English writer for the last decade of his creative life, is also a herald of the modern tradition. In *The Modern Tradition, Backgrounds of Modern Literature*,[9] edited by Richard Ellmann and Charles Feidelson, Jr., the first statement quoted is by Wilde, an extract from 'The Decay of Lying' entitled 'The Priority of Art'; it is interesting that the particular section, 'The Revolt Against Nature', concludes with an extract by André Malraux, 'Art as the Modern Absolute', which, although primarily concerned with painting, might serve as a definition of the goal towards which Wilde was striving. In fact, to see Wilde in a context such as this, alongside Rilke, Mallarmé, Nietzsche, Huysmans, above all Flaubert, as well as Pater, Yeats, Joyce, Eliot, is extremely liberating: an indication of the extent of Wilde's striving, and a confirmation that the grappling with artistic theory, the alignment with European and especially French culture, the confrontation with English values, both in terms of art and morality, are all signs of Wilde's stature.

There are many Wilde texts which continue, and are likely to continue, to command attention: the criticism of *Intentions*, *The Picture of Dorian Gray*, many of the tales, 'The Soul of Man Under Socialism', the comedies, the autobiography of *De Profundis*, *The Ballad of Reading Gaol*. The work, however, which may best indicate the uniqueness of Wilde's achievement is *Salomé*. The degree of experimentation – the initial use of another language, the symbolist form, the approximation to music, the appreciation

of the potential of a particular kind of dance, the visual dimension
– is formidable. What is even more surprising is the probability
that Wilde did not fully appreciate the extent of his achievement
until he was working with Sarah Bernhardt and Graham Robertson; until, perhaps, he accepted that he would never see a fully
realised production. Wilde's struggles with *Salomé* recall the reflections of his master Flaubert:

Meanwhile we are in a shadowy corridor, groping in the dark. We are
without a lever; the ground is slipping under our feet; we all lack a basis
– literati and scribblers that we are. What's the good of all this? Is our
chatter the answer to any need? Between the crowd and ourselves no bond
exists. Alas for the crowd; alas for us, especially. But since there is a
reason for everything, and since the fancy of one individual seems to me
just as valid as the appetite of a million men and can occupy an equal
place in the world, we must (regardless of material things and of
mankind, which disavows us) live for our vocation, climb into our ivory
tower, and dwell there along with our dreams.[10]

Flaubert, too, was tried for offending public morals. Wilde,
prophet of an individual vision, continually left the safety of his
ivory tower and offered that vision, sometimes mockingly from
behind a mask, but sometimes face to face, to the disavowing
crowd.

Notes

The majority of references are to the *Complete Works of Oscar Wilde*, with an introduction by Vyvyan Holland (London, 1966), referred to as *Works*. Other abbreviations are *Letters* (*The Letters of Oscar Wilde*, edited by Rupert Hart-Davis, London, 1962) and *More Letters* (*More Letters of Oscar Wilde*, edited by Hart-Davis, London, 1985).

1 Introduction

1 Walter Pater, *Studies in the History of the Renaissance*, (London, 1873), p. 211.
2 *Works*, p. 522.
3 *Letters*, p. 382.
4 *Works*, p. 901.
5 *Works*, p. 936.
6 *Works*, pp. 936–7.
7 *Works*, p. 1078.
8 *Works*, p. 922.
9 Rodney Shewan, *Oscar Wilde, Art and Egotism* (London, 1977), p. 1.
10 *Letters*, p. 36.
11 *Letters*, p. 41.
12 Vincent O'Sullivan, *Aspects of Wilde* (London, 1936), p. 214.
13 Kenneth Clark, foreword to Stephen Calloway, *Charles Ricketts, Subtle and Fantastic Decorator* (London, 1979), p. 7.
14 Cecil Lewis, ed., *Self-Portrait, Letters and Journals of Charles Ricketts* (London, 1939), pp. 124–5.
15 André Gide, *Oscar Wilde* (London, 1951), pp. 9–10.
16 *Oscar Wilde*, p. 16.
17 *Oscar Wilde*, p. 14.
18 *Oscar Wilde*, p. 29.
19 *Oscar Wilde*, p. 76.
20 *Oscar Wilde*, p. 24.
21 Hesketh Pearson, *The Life of Oscar Wilde* (London, 1946), p. 52.
22 Graham Hough, *The Last Romantics* (London, 1949), p. 199.
23 *Works*, pp. 1058–9.
24 Leon Edel, ed., *Henry James, Letters*, 4 vols (Cambridge, Mass., 1974–84), Vol. 3, p. 373.

2 Oxford and the early poems

1 *Letters*, p. 36.
2 *Letters*, p. 35.
3 *Letters*, p. 36.
4 *More Letters*, p. 25.
5 *Letters*, p. 30–1.
6 *Works*, p. 731.
7 *Letters*, pp. 46–7.
8 'Mr Pater's Last Volume' (*Speaker*, 22 March 1890) in *Collected Works, Reviews*, pp. 538–45.
9 *Works*, pp. 917–18.
10 From 'Mr Oscar Wilde on Mr Oscar Wilde, An Interview' (*St James's Gazette*, 18 January 1895), reproduced in *More Letters*, p. 195.
11 *Collected Works, Reviews*, p. 545.
12 Graham Hough, *The Last Romantics*, p. 137.
13 *The Last Romantics*, p. 137.
14 Walter Pater, *Studies in the History of the Renaissance* (London, 1873), pp. 210–11.
15 Walter Pater, *Marius the Epicurean*, 2 vols (London, 1885), Vol. 1, pp. 35–6.
16 *Works*, p. 32.
17 'Art and the Handicraftsman', *Collected Works, Miscellanies*, pp. 306–7.
18 *Letters*, p. 218.
19 John Ruskin, *The Stones of Venice*, 3 vols (London, 1851–3), Vol. 2, pp. 162–3.
20 *Letters*, p. 61.
21 *Letters*, pp. 62–3.
22 *Letters*, p. 75.
23 *Letters*, p. 70.
24 *Athenaeum*, 23 July 1881, reproduced in Karl Beckson, ed., *Oscar Wilde: The Critical Heritage* (London, 1970), p. 34.
25 *Saturday Review*, 23 July 1881, in *The Critical Heritage*, p. 37.
26 *Academy*, 30 July 1881, in *The Critical Heritage*, p. 40.
27 *Works*, p. 716.
28 *Works*, p. 709.
29 *Works*, p. 719.
30 *Works*, p. 723.
31 *Works*, p. 724.
32 *Works*, p. 736.
33 *Works*, p. 742.
34 *Works*, p. 745.
35 *Works*, p. 769.
36 *Works*, p. 763.
37 *Works*, p. 769.
38 *Works*, p. 770.

39 *Works*, p. 780.
40 *Works*, p. 782.
41 *Works*, p. 784.
42 *Works*, p. 793.
43 *Works*, p. 800.
44 *Works*, p. 801.
45 *Oscar Wilde: Art and Egotism*, pp. 10–11.

3 Lectures and essays

1 *Letters*, pp. 92–3.
2 *Letters*, p. 86.
3 *Letters*, p. 87.
4 *Collected Works, Miscellanies*, p. 262.
5 *Miscellanies*, p. 276.
6 *Letters*, p. 97.
7 *Miscellanies*, p. 244.
8 *Miscellanies*, p. 244.
9 *Miscellanies*, p. 257.
10 *Miscellanies*, p. 263.
11 *Miscellanies*, p. 270.
12 *Miscellanies*, p. 274.
13 *Miscellanies*, p. 277.
14 *Works*, p. 912.
15 Théophile Gautier, *Mademoiselle de Maupin* (Paris, 1835): 'things are beautiful in inverse ratio to their usefulness. Nothing is truly beautiful unless it is useless. Everything useful is ugly.'
16 Théophile Gautier, *Emaux et Camées* (Paris, 1852). Translation by Anthony Hartley, *The Penguin Book of French Verse*, Vol. 3 (London, 1957), p. 138.
17 *Oscar Wilde: Art and Egotism*, p. 82.
18 *Works*, p. 1061.
19 *Works*, p. 1077.
20 *Works*, p. 1078.
21 *Works*, p. 1078.
22 *Letters*, p. 295.
23 *Works*, p. 993.
24 *Works*, p. 995.
25 *Works*, p. 1002.
26 *Works*, p. 1007.
27 *Works*, p. 970.
28 *Works*, p. 992.
29 *Works*, p. 877.
30 *Letters*, p. 428.
31 *Works*, pp. 991–2.
32 *Works*, p. 982.

33 *Works*, p. 975.
34 *Works*, p. 1013.
35 *Works*, p. 1027.
36 *Works*, p. 1034.
37 *Works*, p. 1039.
38 *Works*, p. 1040.
39 *Works*, pp. 1046–7.
40 *Works*, p. 1049.
41 *Works*, p. 1052.
42 *Works*, p. 1053.
43 *Works*, p. 1058.
44 *Works*, p. 1059.
45 *Works*, p. 1089.
46 *Works*, p. 1081.
47 *Works*, p. 1085.
48 *Works*, p. 1086.
49 *Works*, p. 1101.
50 *Works*, p. 1104.
51 *Works*, pp. 922–3.

4 Stories

1 *Collected Works, Reviews*, p. 538.
2 W. B. Yeats on *The Happy Prince and Other Tales*, in *The Critical Heritage*, p. 397.
3 Vyvyan Holland, *Son of Oscar Wilde* (London, 1954), p. 53.
4 *Letters*, p. 233.
5 *Letters*, p. 255.
6 *Letters*, p. 218.
7 *Letters*, p. 219.
8 *Letters*, p. 221.
9 *Letters*, p. 301.
10 W. B. Yeats, *Autobiographies* (London, 1955), p. 135.
11 *Works*, p. 168.
12 *Works*, p. 168.
13 *Works*, p. 172.
14 *Works*, p. 178.
15 *Works*, p. 191.
16 *Works*, p. 192.
17 *Works*, pp. 175–6.
18 *Works*, p. 789.
19 *Works*, p. 176.
20 *Works*, p. 745.
21 For example, Tom Stoppard's *After Magritte* and *The Real Inspector Hound*, or Joe Orton's *What the Butler Saw*.
22 *Works*, p. 205.

23 *Works*, pp. 207–8.
24 *Works*, p. 214.
25 *Works*, p. 194.
26 Isobel Murray, introduction to *The Complete Shorter Fiction of Oscar Wilde* (Oxford, 1979), p. 10.
27 *Works*, p. 291.
28 *Works*, p. 289.
29 *Works*, p. 290.
30 *Works*, p. 293.
31 *Works*, p. 295.
32 *Letters*, p. 218.
33 *Letters*, p. 219.
34 *Works*, p. 299.
35 *Works*, p. 303.
36 *Letters*, p. 237
37 *Letters*, p. 221.
38 *Works*, p. 973.
39 *Works*, p. 991.
40 *Collected Works, Miscellanies*, p. 256.
41 *Works*, p. 309.
42 *Works*, p. 226.
43 *Works*, p. 232.
44 *Works*, p. 237.
45 *Works*, p. 247.
46 *Works*, p. 272.
47 *Works*, p. 284.
48 *Works*, p. 276.
49 *Works*, p. 283.
50 *Letters*, p. 244.
51 *Letters*, p. 366.
52 *Works*, p. 1153.
53 *Works*, p. 1200.
54 *Works*, p. 863.
55 *Works*, p. 866.

5 *The Picture of Dorian Gray*

1 *Letters*, p. 255.
2 *Letters*, p. 257.
3 *Letters*, p. 263.
4 *Letters*, p. 266.
5 *Works*, p. 32.
6 *Works*, p. 34.
7 *Works*, p. 167.
8 *Works*, p. 77.
9 *Works*, p. 133.

10 *Works*, p. 166.
11 *Works*, p. 167.
12 *Works*, p. 53.
13 *Works*, p. 67.
14 *Works*, pp. 67–8.
15 *Works*, p. 68.
16 *Works*, p. 69.
17 *Works*, p. 72.
18 *Works*, p. 73.
19 *Works*, p. 74.
20 *Works*, p. 75.
21 *Works*, p. 81.
22 *Works*, p. 86.
23 *Works*, p. 88.
24 *Works*, p. 94.
25 *Works*, pp. 87–8.
26 *Works*, pp. 57.
27 *Works*, p. 58.
28 *Works*, p. 63.
29 *Works*, p. 57.
30 *Works*, p. 100.
31 *Works*, p. 101.
32 *Letters*, p. 471.
33 *Works*, p. 115.
34 *Works*, pp. 111–12.
35 *Works*, pp. 102–3.
36 *Works*, pp. 126.
37 *Works*, p. 141.
38 *Works*, p. 144.
39 Richard Ellmann, ed., *Letters of James Joyce* (New York, 1966), Vol. 2, p. 150, in *The Critical Heritage*, p. 269.
40 *The Bookman*, November 1891, in *The Critical Heritage*, pp. 83–6.
41 *Letters*, p. 352.
42 *Works*, p. 161.
43 *Works*, pp. 162–3.
44 *Works*, p. 163.
45 *Works*, p. 164.

6 Plays: the social comedies

1 John Russell Taylor, *The Rise and Fall of the Well-made Play* (London, 1967), p. 89.
2 Ada Leverson, 'The Last First Night', *The New Criterion*, January 1926.
3 Squire Bancroft, *Empty Chairs* (London, 1925), p. 112.
4 Hesketh Pearson, *Beerbohm Tree* (London, 1956), p. 67.

5 Gilbert Burgess, '*An Ideal Husband* at the Haymarket Theatre. A Talk with Mr Oscar Wilde', *The Sketch*, 9 January 1895.
6 Arthur Symons, *Plays, Acting and Music* (London, 1903), p. 87.
7 *Letters*, pp. 135–42.
8 *Works*, p. 409.
9 *More Letters*, p. 112.
10 *More Letters*, p. 113.
11 *Letters*, p. 313.
12 *Works*, p. 409.
13 *Works*, p. 388.
14 *Works*, p. 405.
15 Ian Gregor, 'Comedy and Oscar Wilde', *Sewanee Review*, 74:2 (April–June 1966), 501–21, pp. 501, 502.
16 *Works*, p. 416.
17 *Works*, p. 422.
18 *Works*, p. 430.
19 *Works*, p. 387.
20 *Works*, p. 429.
21 *Works*, pp. 397–8.
22 Julia Neilson, *This for Remembrance* (London, 1940), p. 189.
23 Katharine Worth, *Oscar Wilde* (London, 1983), p. 127.
24 *Works*, p. 443.
25 *Works*, p. 442.
26 *Works*, p. 481.
27 *Works*, p. 471.
28 *Works*, p. 469.
29 *Works*, p. 462.
30 Christopher Nassaar, *Into the Demon Universe* (New Haven, Conn., 1974), p. 122.
31 William Archer, *World*, 26 April 1893; also in Archer, *The Theatrical 'World' for 1893*, and *The Critical Heritage*, p. 145.
32 *The Critical Heritage*, p.146.
33 *Works*, p. 483.
34 George Bernard Shaw, *Saturday Review*, 12 January 1895; also in Shaw, *Our Theatres in the Nineties*, and *The Critical Heritage*, p. 177.
35 *Works*, p. 549.
36 *Works*, p. 489.
37 *Works*, p. 499.
38 *Works*, p. 537.
39 *Works*, p. 523.
40 *Letters*, p. 339.
41 *The Critical Heritage*, p. 178.

7 Plays: *Salomé*

1 Wilfrid Scawen Blunt, *My Diaries*, 2 vols (London, 1919), Vol. 1, p. 72.

2 E. H. Mikhail, ed., *Oscar Wilde: Interviews and Recollections*, 2 vols (London, 1979), Vol. 1, p. 188.
3 *Works*, p. 922.
4 *Letters*, p. 590.
5 Philippe Jullian, *Oscar Wilde*, translated by Violet Wyndham (London, 1969), p. 247.
6 *Works*, p. 880.
7 Joris-Karl Huysmans, *A Rebours* (Paris, 1884), translated by Robert Baldick as *Against Nature* (London, 1959), p. 64.
8 *Against Nature*, pp. 65–6.
9 *Against Nature*, pp. 69–70.
10 *Letters*, p. 589.
11 Gustave Flaubert, *Trois Contes*, ed. René Dumesnil (Paris, 1957), pp. 128–9.
12 *Stéphane Mallarmé*, translated by Anthony Hartley (London, 1965), p. 40.
13 Katharine Worth, *Oscar Wilde*, p. 55.
14 Maurice Maeterlinck, *Théâtre Complet*, 3 vols (Brussels and Paris, 1901–2), Vol. 1, p. 5.
15 *Collected Works, Salomé, A Florentine Tragedy and Vera*, p. 5.
16 *Letters*, p. 757.
17 *Letters*, p. 136.
18 *Works*, p. 553.
19 *Works*, p. 555.
20 *Works*, p. 558.
21 *Works*, p. 560.
22 *Works*, p. 562.
23 *Works*, p. 566.
24 *Works*, p. 569.
25 *Works*, p. 571.
26 *Works*, p. 573.
27 Frank Kermode, *Romantic Image* (London, 1957), pp. 73–4.
28 William Butler Yeats, *Collected Plays*, 2nd edition (London, 1952), p. 694.
29 W. Graham Robertson, *Time Was* (London, 1931), p. 126.
30 Charles Ricketts, *Oscar Wilde: Recollections by Jean Paul Raymond and Charles Ricketts* (London, 1932), p. 53.
31 *Letters*, p. 834.
32 *Time Was*, p. 127.
33 Cecil Lewis, ed., *Self-Portrait*, p. 137.
34 Charles Ricketts, *Pages on Art* (London, 1913), p. 244.
35 *Self-Portrait*, p. 137.
36 *Self-Portrait*, p. 137.
37 *Self-Portrait*, p. 319.

8 Plays: *The Importance of Being Earnest*

1 *Letters*, p. 382.
2 W. H. Auden, 'An Improbable Life: Review of Letters of Oscar Wilde', *New Yorker*, 9 March 1963; also in Richard Ellmann, ed., *Oscar Wilde: A Collection of Critical Essays* (Englewood Cliffs, N.J., 1969), pp. 116–37.
3 G. B. Shaw, *Saturday Review*, 23 February 1895; also in *The Critical Heritage*, pp. 194–5.
4 William Archer, *World*, 20 February 1895; also in *The Theatrical 'World' of 1895*, pp. 56–60, and *The Critical Heritage*, pp. 189–91.
5 *Letters*, p. 376.
6 Mary McCarthy, *Sights and Spectacles* (London, 1959), p. 105; also in *Oscar Wilde: A Collection of Critical Essays*, pp. 107–10.
7 *Works*, p. 365.
8 John Gielgud, *An Actor and His Time* (London, 1979), p. 158.
9 *Works*, p. 368.
10 *Works*, p. 370.
11 *Works*, p. 380.
12 *Works*, p. 345.
13 *Works*, p. 374.
14 *Works*, p. 379.
15 *Works*, p. 371.
16 G. B. Shaw, 'My Memories of Oscar Wilde', in *Oscar Wilde: A Collection of Critical Essays*, pp. 95–6.
17 Katharine Worth, *Oscar Wilde*, p. 179.
18 *Works*, p. 321.
19 *Works*, p. 322.
20 *Works*, p. 332.
21 *Works*, p. 334.
22 *Works*, p. 372.

9 *De Profundis* and *The Ballad of Reading Gaol*

1 *Letters*, pp. 423–4.
2 *Works*, p. 956.
3 *Letters*, p. 512.
4 *Letters*, p. 513.
5 *Works*, p. 951.
6 *Works*, p. 892.
7 *Works*, p. 884.
8 *Works*, p. 874.
9 *Works*, p. 909
10 *Works*, p. 912.
11 *Works*, p. 913.
12 *Works*, p. 919.

13 *Works*, p. 920.
14 *Works*, p. 928.
15 *Works*, p. 906.
16 *Works*, p. 915.
17 *Works*, p. 916.
18 *Works*, p. 929.
19 *Works*, p. 933.
20 *Works*, p. 938.
21 *Works*, p. 931.
22 *Works*, p. 928.
23 *Works*, p. 284.
24 *Works*, p. 955.
25 *Works*, p. 956.
26 *Works*, p. 957.
27 *Letters*, p. 654.
28 *More Letters*, p. 150.
29 W. E. Henley, *Outlook*, 5 March 1898, in *The Critical Heritage*, p. 216.
30 First published in *The Gem*, 1829.
31 *Letters*, p. 654.
32 *Works*, p. 848.
33 *The Critical Heritage*, p. 215.
34 Arthur Symons, *Saturday Review*, 12 March 1898, in *The Critical Heritage*, p. 221.
35 W. B. Yeats in *The Critical Heritage*, p. 397.

10 Conclusion

1 Letter to Frank Harris in *Pearson's Magazine*, March 1918, in *The Critical Heritage*, pp. 384–5.
2 Holbrook Jackson, *The Eighteen Nineties* (London, 1913), pp. 72–90, and in *The Critical Heritage*, pp. 325–39.
3 J. Cowper Powys, *Suspended Judgments* (New York, 1916), pp. 401–22, and in *The Critical Heritage*, pp. 355–65.
4 *Oscar Wilde: Art and Egotism*, p. 202.
5 Jorge Luis Borges, 'About Oscar Wilde', in *Oscar Wilde: A Collection of Critical Essays*, p. 174.
6 Robert Baldick, ed., *Pages from the Goncourt Journal* (Oxford, 1962), p. 24.
7 *Oscar Wilde: A Collection of Critical Essays*, p. 174.
8 Leon Edel, ed., *Henry James, Letters*, Vol. 3, p. 373.
9 Richard Ellmann and Charles Feidelson, Jr., eds., *The Modern Tradition, Backgrounds of Modern Literature* (New York, 1965).
10 Francis Steegmuller, trans., *Selected Letters of Gustave Flaubert* (London, 1954), p. 133.

Select bibliography

The following bibliography represents a selection of the most useful critical editions of Wilde's works, and a number of biographical and critical books. I have not repeated all the references in the endnotes, only the major sources and those that I have found most useful.

Wilde's works

Collected Edition of the Works of Oscar Wilde, ed. Robert Ross, 15 vols. (London, 1908; reprinted 1969).

Complete Works of Oscar Wilde, introduction by Vyvyan Holland (London, 1966).

The Artist as Critic: Critical Writings of Oscar Wilde, ed. Richard Ellmann (New York, 1969; London, 1972).

The Complete Shorter Fiction of Oscar Wilde, ed. Isobel Murray (Oxford, 1979).

The Importance of Being Earnest, ed. Russell Jackson (London, 1980).

Lady Windermere's Fan, ed. Ian Small (London, 1980).

The Picture of Dorian Gray, ed. Isobel Murray (Oxford, 1974).

Two Society Comedies, ed. Ian Small and Russell Jackson (London, 1983).

Bibliographical and biographical sources

Fletcher, Ian and Stokes, John, 'Oscar Wilde', *Anglo-Irish Literature: A Guide to Research* (Modern Language Association of America, 1976).

Mason, Stuart, *A Bibliography of Oscar Wilde* (London, 1916; reissued, 1967).

Mikhail, E. H., *Oscar Wilde: An Annotated Bibliography of Criticism* (London, 1978).

Ellmann, Richard, *Oscar Wilde* (London, 1987).

Hart-Davis, Rupert, ed., *The Letters of Oscar Wilde* (London, 1962).

More Letters of Oscar Wilde (London, 1985).

Holland, Vyvyan, *Oscar Wilde and His World* (London, 1978).

Hyde, H. Montgomery, *The Trials of Oscar Wilde* (London, 1960).

Oscar Wilde (London, 1976).

Mikhail, E. H., ed., *Oscar Wilde: Interviews and Recollections*, 2 vols. (London, 1979).

Pearson, Hesketh, *The Life of Oscar Wilde* (London, 1946; revised edition, 1954).

159

SELECT BIBLIOGRAPHY

Major criticism

Beckson, Karl, ed., *Oscar Wilde: The Critical Heritage* (London, 1970).
Bird, Alan, *The Plays of Oscar Wilde* (London, 1977).
Cohen, Philip K., *The Moral Vision of Oscar Wilde* (Cranberry, N.J., 1979).
Ellmann, Richard, ed., *Oscar Wilde: A Collection of Critical Essays* (Englewood Cliffs, N.J., 1969).
Ervine, St John, *Oscar Wilde: A Present Time Appraisal* (London, 1951).
Gide, André, *Oscar Wilde* (London, 1951).
Kohl, Norbert, *Oscar Wilde: The Works of a Conformist Rebel* (Cambridge, 1988).
Nassaar, Christopher, *Into the Demon Universe: A Literary Exploration of Oscar Wilde* (Yale, 1974).
Roditi, Edouard, *Oscar Wilde* (Norfolk, Conn., 1947).
San Juan Jr., Epifanio, *The Art of Oscar Wilde* (Princeton, 1967).
Shewan, Rodney, *Oscar Wilde: Art and Egotism* (London, 1977).
Sullivan, Kevin, *Oscar Wilde* (New York, 1972).
Symons, Arthur, *A Study of Oscar Wilde* (London, 1930).
Tydeman, William, ed., *Wilde, Comedies: A Selection of Critical Essays* (London, 1982).
Woodcock, George, *The Paradox of Oscar Wilde* (London and New York, 1949).
Worth, Katharine, *Oscar Wilde*, Macmillan Modern Dramatists (London, 1983).

(The three volumes edited by Karl Beckson, Richard Ellmann and William Tydeman bring together a considerable range of historical and modern material, including reviews, letters, articles, essays and extracts from longer works of criticism.)

Further criticism

Archer, William, *The Theatrical 'World' of 1893–7* (London, 1894–8).
Fletcher, Ian, *Romantic Mythologies* (London, 1967).
    ed., *Decadence and the 1890s*, Stratford-upon-Avon Studies, 17 (London, 1979).
Hough, Graham, *The Last Romantics* (London, 1949).
Jackson, Holbrook, *The Eighteen Nineties* (London, 1927).
Kermode, Frank, *Romantic Image* (London, 1957).
Mason, Stuart, *Oscar Wilde and the Aesthetic Movement* (London, 1920).
Praz, Mario, *The Romantic Agony* (London, 1954).
Ricketts, Charles (originally issued under the pseudonym of J. P. Raymond), *Oscar Wilde: Recollections by Jean Paul Raymond and Charles Ricketts* (London, 1932).
Worth, Katharine, *The Irish Drama of Europe from Yeats to Beckett* (London, 1978).

Index

A Rebours (Huysmans), 35, 75, 102–4
Adey, More, 132–3
Alexander II, Czar of Russia, 82
Alexander, George, 81, 83–4, 120–1, 129
Allan, Maud, 118
Andersen, Hans Christian, 57, 63
Anderson, Mary, 35, 38, 82, 106
Appreciations (Pater), 15
Archer, William, 95, 120
Arnold, Matthew, 17, 23, 26, 63
As You Like It (Shakespeare), 38, 73
At The Hawk's Well (Yeats), 115
Atta Troll (Heine), 114
Auden, W. H., 120

Balzac, Honoré de, 12, 35, 42
Bancroft, Lady, 81
Baudelaire, Charles, 9, 33, 35–37, 65, 139
Beardsley, Aubrey, 102, 144
Beckett, Samuel, 10, 66, 101, 131
Beere, Mrs Bernard, 82
Berlioz, Hector, 73
Bernhardt, Sarah, 22, 116, 148
Bible, the, 56, 108, 111, 136–8
Blackwood, William, 64
Blunt, Wilfred Scawen, 101
Borges, Jorge Luis, 144, 146
Boucicault, Dion, 31, 86
Brand (Ibsen), 4
Browning, Oscar, 23
Brummell, Beau, 35
Buchan, John, 76
Burne-Jones, Edward, 24, 139
Butler, Samuel, 121
Byron, Lord, 5, 9, 24, 135, 137

Campbell, Lady Archibald, 38, 73
Carte, Richard D'Oyly, 12, 31
Case of Rebellious Susan, The (Jones), 121
Cenci, The (Shelley), 82
Chekhov, Anton, 91
Chesterton, G. K., 146
Colegate, Isabel, 74
Coleridge, S.T., 55, 141

Colonel, The (Burnand), 22
Congreve, William, 86, 125
Craig, Gordon, 38–9
Crane, Walter, 56

Dandy, The (Baudelaire), 35
Dante, 139
Darragh, Miss, 118
Darwin, Charles, 45–6
D'Aurevilly, Jules, 35
Death of Cuchulain, The (Yeats), 115–16
Degas, Edgar, 35, 116
Dickens, Charles, 31
Dilke, Sir Charles, 22
Disraeli, Benjamin, 13, 40, 97
Divine Comedy (Dante), 139
Donne, John, 9
Doré, Gustave, 13
Douglas, Lord Alfred, 1, 3, 7–8, 102, 104, 121, 132–4, 139–40
Dream of Eugene Aram, The (Hood), 141
Du Dandysme (D'Aurevilly), 35
Dumas, Alexandre, fils, 3, 9, 85–6, 96
Du Maurier, George, 22
Duse, Eleonora, 118

Earthly Paradise, The (Morris), 27
Eliot, T. S., 147
Elton, Oliver, 9
Emaux et Camées (Gautier), 36, 76–7
Endgame (Beckett), 66
Entertainer, The (Osborne), 91
Etherege, George, 86

Fanfarlo, La (Baudelaire), 73
Festival Theatre, Cambridge, 118
Flaubert, Gustave, 9, 16, 36–7, 46, 49, 58, 64–5, 75, 104, 146–8
Fleurs du Mal, Les (Baudelaire), 139
Francis of Assisi, 139
Full Moon in March, A (Yeats), 115

Gaston de Latour (Pater), 16

161

INDEX

162

INDEX

163

INDEX

VILLA JULIE COLLEGE LIBRARY
GREEN SPRING VALLEY ROAD
STEVENSON, MD   21153